PENNSYLVANIA
GOOD EATS

PENNSYLVANIA
GOOD EATS

EXPLORING THE STATE'S FAVORITE, UNIQUE, HISTORIC, AND DELICIOUS FOODS

TEXT AND PHOTOS BY
BRIAN YARVIN

Globe
Pequot

Guilford, Connecticut

Globe Pequot

An imprint of Globe Pequot, the trade division of
The Rowman & Littlefield Publishing Group, Inc.
4501 Forbes Blvd., Ste. 200
Lanham, MD 20706
www.rowman.com

Distributed by NATIONAL BOOK NETWORK

British Library Cataloguing in Publication Information available
Library of Congress Cataloging-in-Publication Data available

ISBN 978-1-4930-5571-5 (paper : alk. paper)
ISBN 978-1-4930-5572-2 (electronic)

♾™ The paper used in this publication meets the minimum requirements of
American National Standard for Information Sciences—Permanence of Paper for
Printed Library Materials, ANSI/NISO Z39.48-1992.

Contents

Pennsylvania: Where No Food Is Forgotten

In Pennsylvania, a short drive down any narrow road will bring you to neighborhoods, towns, forests, and farms that have not changed in decades. It is so filled with nooks and crannies that any food, no matter how archaic or obscure, can find an out-of-the-way place to thrive. Techniques that your grandparents used are still out there in a village, farm, or shop somewhere. Anytime you hear somebody say, "Nobody cooks that anymore!" you can be sure that somebody in the Keystone State is preparing it.

Historic dishes like scrapple and buckwheat cakes form part of an edible record. Smoked sausages, fried noodles, and the component parts of a pizza are all history on a plate. Where do you find these things? And what makes them great? In order to discover the answers, we'll have to leave the kitchen and hit the road.

The broad range of Pennsylvania places, from city to wilderness, works in our favor. A more rural region would never be able to sustain all those immigrant and specialty sources. If we were more urban, then

One of the many versions of pork and sauerkraut, a Pennsylvania Dutch New Year's Day classic

A bowl of chicken corn noodle soup, a Pennsylvania Dutch Classic

Red beet eggs, hard boiled eggs cooked in red beet juice, a Pennsylvania Dutch favorite

we'd lose the contributions of farmers and the traditions they carry. College towns bring in the newest and the hippest, and suburbs have a way of working all those factors into a uniform whole. Tacos, scrapple, and heirloom tomatoes are all part of our collective food culture.

I have spent an awful lot of time exploring Pennsylvania. I drove, I hiked, I took a few trains, and I ate—a lot. If you do the same, you will quickly realize there is no "best." And, luckily, no worst either. What we do have are places that are more iconic, or more authentic, or maybe even more eccentric. I sought them all out.

If a destination was open to the public, I came without calling. I always visited as a customer, and described myself as a "writer and photographer" only when I had difficult questions or wanted to take pictures with a pro camera. So, for the most part, my experience is your experience. I talked doughnuts while I waited in line at Oram's (see p. 147) and chatted with the crowd at the Dutch Eating Place (see p. 172).

On rare occasions, special arrangements were made. For example, at Valley Milkhouse (see p. 208), I took (and paid for) a cheese-making workshop. I did the whole class from beginning to end and stuck my arms in the milk vat up to my elbows. Indeed, I took every tour and every workshop I possibly could. Sometimes I just showed up. It was not idealism that made me work this way. Rather, it was the fact that almost nobody I called was interested in talking. For a long while, showing up was the only strategy.

This changed in a big way when the Covid-19 Pandemic hit. Because we were all stuck at home, I was suddenly able to conduct serious interviews by phone. Farmers and artisans that wouldn't normally give a stranger the time of day were ready to share their lives. I changed too; I was no longer saying "the food tells the story." Instead, the creators themselves were doing the talking.

There is a lot more here than Pennsylvania Dutch. In Pittston, where the Italian flag flies in the center of town, neon signs in restaurant windows boast "we have tripe!" or "Italian Spaghetti." It is one of the many ways the foods of immigrant coal miners remain alive. In the town of Shenandoah, less than sixty miles away, the word "sausage" means kielbasa. There the cuisine is Polish, but both share a history of mines and forests that is purely Pennsylvanian.

When you are out there at a market or festival, you get the feeling this is the place where somebody or other remembers everything. Yes, that somebody not only remembers the difference between souse and head cheese, but they are also still making it using their great-grandfather's recipe. Was that recipe created in Romania? Italy? Vietnam? Or maybe even right down the road. Wherever it came from, it is waiting for you, surprised that you are surprised to see it.

Modern immigrants are having their days too. Visit the authentic Chinese restaurants popping up in college towns—often enough, they are right down the road from eateries that serve food from Korea and Thailand and mixed with places that offer the cuisines of Latin America. Of course, there could be burgers and waffles right next door.

A couple of fasnachts, the Pennsylvania Dutch Lenten doughnuts

Pennsylvania's farmers are hardly idle. They are growing, preserving, and creating too. Check out crops as traditional as fresh corn, as trendy as kale, or as esoteric as *waygu* beef. We each can have our own adventures and make our own discoveries. The classics remain, the old is preserved, and newcomers bring their own contributions. Some of it may be hidden, and everybody is willing to share.

This book is a snapshot of a vast and rapidly changing food culture. I hope it is a good starting point for your own food adventures; all I ask is that you do not forget it is a starting point and nothing more. We are a whole state that is being recycled, up-cycled, and re-invented. A challenge is out there—can we embrace all this food? Can we know it? Love it? And yes, eat it?

Let's explore, taste, and learn.

ALABASTER COFFEE ROASTER & TEA CO

LYCOMING COUNTY
400 PINE ST., WILLIAMSPORT, PA 17701;
ALABASTERCOFFEE.COM; (570) 478-0043

Standing at the counter at Alabaster Coffee in Williamsport, I could not help but notice that the cup intended for my drink was filled with plain boiling water. You may think it was meant for somebody else: maybe it would get a tea bag or maybe it would be served as-is to somebody who drank their boiling water neat, Chinese style. As it turns out, that cup was being warmed up while my coffee was brewing. When it was served, coffee and cup were both at the same temperature.

This was astounding attention to detail! Just what you would expect at a top-notch shop in London, Tokyo, or New York, but like everything else at Alabaster, it seemed at bit out of place. I thought I knew Williamsport, an isolated lumber town that was home to Little League Baseball. And with that cup of coffee, Alabaster put Williamsport on the serious coffee map too.

Alabaster claims to build community through coffee. I did not see any trace of it though. However, there was easily enough going on; fresh, bright, fruity cups for the serious, and specialty drinks for the rest. Sharp eyes could notice different grinders for brewed and espresso coffees and a fully manual espresso machine—you would have to be something of an expert to operate it and a deeper sort of aficionado to appreciate that it was there.

I could tell the difference, I enjoyed getting coffee of this quality, and I saw myself as a snob for being this way. I sat down with my pour-over cup at a prime seat by a picture window looking out on downtown Williamsport. The streets were filled with cars and trucks zipping by and the sidewalks were pretty much empty.

There is a wide range of coffees available at Alabaster. They make those drinks from them, and they sell them as beans too. Some are from Latin America; others from Asia, and the one I chose came from Ethiopia. I would take a sip, enjoy this very special brew, and look out the window at the unpopulated city in front of me. Sometimes somebody would walk by. A lawyer? An accountant? I would sip some more and think about it.

A cup of coffee from Alabaster with a cookie in the background

The two baristas both knew their coffee and the town. They were "from there," had grown up there, and learned their coffee someplace else. I tried to find out about their interests in the specialty coffee world. They had degrees in other subjects and had turned their back on them. Instead, they were here in this dead quiet store, selling some of the finest coffee in the state.

It was another of those gastronomic islands. I had washed ashore in this lonely place where the only attraction was this coffee. I sipped until there was nothing but a few drops at the bottom of the mug, and then I did my best to suck those drops down. Leaving was like leaving an island too. Williamsport is a long way from anywhere and your journey home is likely to be through some really lonesome country.

When I finished, I walked past a woman roasting small batches of coffee beans and toward my parked car. I could not imagine coming here for a special trip, but if you are on I-80 or Route 15—both big roads between big places—this is where to take a serious break.

ALLENTOWN FAIRGROUNDS MARKET

LEHIGH COUNTY
1825 CHEW ST., ALLENTOWN, PA 18104;
ALLENTOWNFARMERSMARKET.COM; (610) 432-8425

What are you going to eat when you visit the Allentown Fairgrounds Market? Even though this is not a food court in the sense of the market houses in Harrisburg (see p. 31) or Philadelphia (see p. 84, 167), there are still some serious choices. Vietnamese and Irish are almost elbow to elbow. Korean and Pennsylvania Dutch sit facing each other across a very narrow aisle. And a Greek vendor a few steps away works the crowd under a banner that implores you to "taste the power of garlic and olive oil."

This market caters to relatively poor customers with food that a far more affluent audience could only dream of. Quality produce, grass-fed meats, artisan sausages, and baked goods too. What you can find here is what urban food activists are talking about—wholesome food sold by local retailers at reasonable prices.

Pennsylvania does not have night markets filled with vendors the way so many cities around the world do. We have markets though—we

A perfect hot lunch—chicken pot pie from the Allentown Fairgrounds Market

3

Bunches of asparagus for sale at a produce stand in the Allentown Fairgrounds Market

call them "market houses"—and they are our take on the best way to find great food. You may be looking for string beans, a bowl of soup, or a sack of potatoes; market houses will have them.

Even when you are not looking for something, a market house visit will be a window on the local community.

Uniquely located under the grandstands of a stadium, the Allentown Fairgrounds Market tells you the story of a town in food and culture. The first words I heard spoken as I walked in the door were in Polish. They came from behind a stand selling cured sausages and freshly made pierogies. the Lancaster Central Market (see p. 112) will be delighted to tell the town story. Others, like the Allentown Fairgrounds Market, are discreet enough to let you make discoveries yourself.

I ate my share of junk food that day. A doughnut and a pretzel-wrapped hot dog too. They bracketed the most wholesome lunch imaginable—a chicken pot pie. Not the Pennsylvania Dutch–style stew, an actual pie with crust on top and meat, sauce, and vegetables inside.

This may not be in the middle of Pennsylvania Dutch Country, but there is sure lots of scrapple here. Indeed, the butchers were the most impressive category. Since this was my sixth or seventh market house visit of the book, I was noticing a trend in butchering—the poorer the neighborhood, the better the bones. At the Allentown Fairgrounds Market, both the steaks and the bones were worth a second look. Some really formidable cooks must shop here.

Seller after seller kept attracting my attention, there was one offering "southern" as a cuisine. I looked longingly at the meatloaf, baked beans, and banana pudding and then saw a fresh poultry case with rabbit and stewing hens a few steps away. Then the tamales, then the pies, then, then, then . . .

Luckily, I was too broke to buy anything, or maybe broke enough to think hard before I shelled out. "Gourmet" here seemed to mean "the same as a supermarket deli case," while goose and capon did not seem to require any adjectives at all. Indeed, there was not a trace of luxury or pretense in the place. You could buy fillet mignon here, and pork necks too. It is a market house where you can come and eat, but also one you can also appreciate if you do the cooking.

AMAZING ACRES GOAT DAIRY

CHESTER COUNTY
AVAILABLE AT LOCAL STORES AND FARMERS MARKETS;
AMAZINGACRESGOATSDAIRY.COM

Sometimes, when I hear someone describe a place as amazing, I yawn and sort of ask, why? And equally often, I will think the existence of any farm this close to Philadelphia is amazing in itself. When it comes to the Amazing Acres Goat Dairy in Elverson, there is something even more amazing—the way owners Will and Lynn Reid went from an adult ed class in cheese making to farm ownership in a very short time.

They studied cheese for a while, and then somehow found themselves owning a five-acre goat farm. Neither of them had the slightest experience in any of this. No farming in their past, no childhood memories of summers on the family goat pasture, no background at all. Somebody else called it Amazing Acres before they bought it and Will does not remember if he was ever told why.

This is one of those places that does not do many different things, but what they do is remarkable. Will and Lynn started with fresh goat cheeses; the ones that are soft and spreadable. There is good reason for this—they are simple enough to make and can be brought to nearby "Main Line" farmers' markets while they are still very fresh.

It was a wise beginning. While other farmers try to fill their shelves with aged cheeses like cheddar or tomme, Amazing Acres could comfortably turn out enough soft cheese to make trips to farmers' markets worthwhile. They were *chèvres*—that is the French word for goat cheese, and in Southeastern Pennsylvania, a word like that conveys sophistication.

When they had enough milking goats, they decided to expand their line. Instead of the cave-aged products that most local cheese makers aspire to, Will took a stab at bloomy-rind. They are the ones with textured white skins. Those of you who entertained back in the seventies will remember the most famous bloomy rind of them all: brie.

Brie was the first imported cheese that Americans loved in a big way. Today, histories of brie and other bloomy-rind cheeses concentrate on France with stories of kings and peasants. In my universe, brie was one of the first foods you could serve that marked you as cool.

Fifty years ago, articles in men's magazines like *Esquire* and *Playboy* spilled torrents of words telling readers how to properly choose one and local newspapers like the *Village Voice* told you where to find them.

It worked (at least for me), serving a brie or bringing one as a gift marked me as a true hip New Yorker. I would go to tiny stores in Manhattan's East Village and buy brie a dozen at a time, just to make sure I was ready.

People have different expectations nowadays. The brie I found in 1977 may have given me something of a social life, but it was not half as good as what is sold in chain supermarkets today. Will and Lynn face a different problem. They must make a cheese that justifies the hefty price they need to charge to stay afloat. Once again, "amazing" is the key word. At the markets they sell at, customers expect something every bit as good as the best they had in France—or at least in one of Philadelphia's grand French restaurants. They have to either deliver or find another career. They deliver.

Inoculated with bacteria, the cheese forms the classic textured white skin. The bloomy-rind process requires impeccable cleanliness and great precision. They pasteurize their own milk, this allows better flavor and texture. They also maintain a separate aging area. As they have become more experienced, they have moved away from brie and are now working on their own recipes. You will have to visit them at one of the farmers' markets to find out what their current creations are.

With Will as cheese maker and Lynn as goat keeper, they are at a sort of impasse. They are producing as much as they can without hiring help and that is it. If they bring somebody on, they will have to have many more goats, just to make payroll. If they do it themselves, they cannot milk even one more.

So that is it, Will and Lynn, five acres at the edge of suburbia, and some goats. In one way, it is not much of anything, and in another, it is a platform for the highest level of artisanship.

APPEL VALLEY BUTCHER SHOP

LANCASTER COUNTY
531 BEAVER VALLEY PIKE, LANCASTER, PA 17602;
REALLANCASTERCOUNTY.COM/APPEL-VALLEY-BUTCHER-SHOP;
(717) 947-4241

Be different!

Instead of walking through the front door at Appel Valley Butcher Shop and heading straight for the steaks the way most people do, check out the bolognas instead. They are brown, in a corner, and kind of shy. While everybody else is hypnotized by the brilliant color of properly presented beef, that bologna wants you just as much and cannot quite put on the same sort of show. House-made from a recipe that twists traditional technique with owner Steve Appel's personal vision of how an artisan sausage should be made, it is the story of the shop stuffed into a real, natural casing.

Do not be fooled by the Lancaster address, Appel Valley Butcher Shop is a tiny business at a rural crossroads. It is a small brick building right behind a private home with a few parking spaces out front—the sort of country store you would expect to find in rural Lancaster county. Step inside and you will find charming and enthusiastic salespeople behind the counter and Steve himself cutting and chopping the beef and pork they sell.

There is even more action on the days they are closed. They make those bolognas of course, and their own bacon and jerky too—all in a smokehouse that dates back to the era of steam locomotives. Steve also spends that quiet shop time breaking down sides and quarters of beef and pork and turning them into those retail items that cry out to you if you make the mistake of coming in without a written shopping list.

The store may only have been called Appel Valley for the past few years, but there has been a butcher here for decades longer. The previous owner, Bob Howry, had been a fixture both here and at the Lancaster Central Market (see p. 112). He was a master! And sadly, a bit too old to have seen the revival of food artisanship that has taken hold around the state.

Steve had been a customer of Bob's for a while before he started dropping hints about buying the place. Bob did not accept the first

Signs point the way to the Appel Valley Butcher Shop outside Lancaster

offer, or the second one either. A few years down the road, things worked out and Steve and his wife were the owners. The Appel family had bought a business and a history too. Not only was there an old, functioning butcher shop, there were Howry's recipes and even the actual stand that was used in the Lancaster Central Market all those years ago.

Artisan butchering is more than just the fancy stuff. As Steve says, "If you take a lousy piece of meat and cut it the right way, you can have a good piece of meat . . . if you take a fantastic piece of prime meat and cut it wrong, you will make it lousy." This does not mean you can cook that properly cut piece any way you feel like it. Someone could (theoretically) cut a roast into steaks and wind up with a finished dish that looked great and was so tough it could not be eaten.

Foods to Look For: Bologna

Few towns in Pennsylvania bring in the New Year with a bologna the way Lebanon does. There, over the last quarter century or so, bolognas that have weighed anything from fifteen pounds to over one hundred pounds have done the job. And yet those "Lebanon Bolognas" are nothing like what most Americans would think of as "bologna." For the rest of us, it is a tender and light pink cooked sausage sliced thinly and usually eaten in sandwiches; something like an Italian *mortadella*. Lebanon Bolognas are more like salamis though. They are dark red and marbled with chunks of ivory fat. Looking at them, you would think they were from Poland or Germany, but one taste tells a whole different story—sweetness that startles.

When you buy them, try to find a shop that has a few whole ones on hand so you can see where they came from. Ideally, they will make their own, but even the biggest brands are still tiny when you compare them to the industrial producers of supermarket cold cuts. In Pennsylvania Dutch Country, they can show up anywhere. In sandwiches of course, for snacks, and as an ingredient in recipes too. Bologna is a staple food.

Bologna is not the only sausage we eat. Every country that has sent immigrants to the Keystone State has its own tradition of sausage making. First there were the Pennsylvania Dutch, and then soon after, butchers from Italy and Eastern Europe added to the repertoire. They could not help mixing and innovating—there was a bounty of ingredients and cultures too. We are truly a state of sausage eaters.

Here's the definition; ground up meat, seasonings, and "extenders" stuffed into tubular cases, often made from intestines. That meat is usually pork, but can also be turkey, chicken, beef, or lamb. Seasonings are salt—often too much salt—and hopefully garlic too. (Although there rarely seems to be enough.) Sometimes you will find spices like oregano in Italian-style or chili in more contemporary renditions.

I urge you to avoid anything that is too far from this ideal, sausage in itself is a flavor—it does not need more. In my opinion, the worst offenders are those filled with cheese. If you love cheese with your sausage, put a piece of it on top while it is cooking.

Hot bologna from Kowalonek's in Shenandoah

And then there are those "extenders." Just cheap fillers meant to stretch the meat out. Any added flour, meal, or starch should be reason to not buy a Pennsylvania product. The exception is blood sausage; British black pudding, Korean *Soodae*, Spanish *Morcilla*, and Polish *Kishka* all have grain added to solidify the filling.

There is a dream those of us who shop from roadside farm stands indulge in; we drive up to a farm that may have nothing but a few baskets of apples on display, but despite the lack of signage, the fragrance of wood smoke tells us another story altogether. Soon the owner is bringing out sausage for you to try and the taste leaves you swooning.

That does not happen very often. Modern standards of hygiene have changed the narrative a bit. Instead, those smoked and cured meats have moved to small butcher shops and market houses. Every corner of the state has local examples. While some butchers may specialize, others try for variety. You may find smoked ring bolognas, fresh Italian sausage, breakfast links, and those skinny dried meat sticks too. Somehow, they have all become Pennsylvanian.

Sometimes shops specialize. Indeed, there is the whole town of Shenandoah (see p. 188) that focuses on traditional Polish, while the area around Old Forge (see p. 144) and Pittston has shops that have quality Italian. Dietrich's Meats & Country Store (see p. 58) is a kind of mecca of meat curing too. Do not limit yourself to these spots though, butcher shops and sausage makers may not be prominent, but they are there.

Sausages are more than cold cuts! Stew fresh sausages in wine or tomato sauce or broil them in your oven. Because their flavors are so strong, you do not have to eat that much. They can be the main course, an appetizer, or even just a seasoning. However, you eat them, they tell our story in every bite.

You know the old question, "What kind of meat does the butcher eat?" I was talking to one and had to ask. Steve likes a nice thick rib eye or a skirt steak for starters. That seemed to be a banal answer for a real beef fan, so I pressed him a bit more. Soon he was talking about the bolar roast. I had never heard of it and should have. It turns out to be a sort of chuck—a big, bone-in cut that is perfect for braising or slow-cooking.

Although the shop may look like it is at a lonely country cross-roads, it is really in a perfect spot. It is near enough to downtown for residents to hop on over and right by the main road to Baltimore. People come in and stock up. Sixty pounds of ground beef? They will grind it for you. A few slices of house-made lunch meat? No problem.

Head on in. Somebody will ask for a pound of sausage and the crew will answer back with, "How about two pounds?" Another customer will ask for pork chops and suddenly, ham samples are being passed around to everybody in the store. There is the smell of smoke-house, the glow of refrigerated cases, and the banter of the Appel family. Meat fans can really call it home.

ASIA MALL

DAUPHIN COUNTY
1030 S. 13TH ST., HARRISBURG, PA 17104;
(717) 232-6019

I was doing some serious studying. Two-inch-high lettering at the base of a refrigerator case read, "Uteri, stomach, blood, liver." Inside were unmarked packages of animal parts that were sort of grouped above the signs. I tried to match the words to them, and it was not working. I spotted some kidneys and they were not mentioned anywhere. Was this a veterinary anatomy pop quiz? Nope. It was the meat department at the Asia Mall in Harrisburg, the perfect place for cooks who miss the choices they had in Vietnam or Thailand. For the rest of us, it is a serious test of our gastronomic skills.

I spotted the blood easily; it was congealed into cakes and sort of like extra credit. This was a compelling Asian grocery, certainly the best in Central Pennsylvania, but all I could think of when I looked at that case of offal was a haggis. Just when I thought my lesson in anatomy was done, I was thrust into one on comparative food cultures—forced to remember what people ate before we had the luxury of exporting (or just trashing) large portions of the animals we slaughter as part of our food supply.

That was the story at the Asia Mall. I had no choice but to approach it with an open mind. It was way too big to be one of those tiny pan-Asian stores you see in other small Pennsylvania cities, and still somehow too small to be thought of as a megastore. None of this prepared me for what I found—aisle after aisle of the Asian grocery standbys punctuated with things I never would have expected.

As I stood there and contemplated the whole notion of food ethics, I came to realize that I too was being stared at by a very big fish. It was a catfish the size of a truck transmission, yet another reminder of the human place on the food chain. Surprises lurk at the Asian Mall. It is a place where you find foods you think you may know offered in forms that you never knew existed.

I took refuge in the pasta department where they seemingly stocked noodles from every corner of Asia. Of course, there were the Chinese and Japanese classics. And one of my biggest finds—plain instant ramen without the seasoning packets. You see them sold this way at street food stalls in Asia, but almost never here. I bought them right away.

Flavored instant ramen noodles are among the most popular and you will find a huge assortment of them here. If you know one of those people who eats nothing else, you can get them twenty or thirty different kinds and vastly expand their diet without taking away the basics.

Keep shopping! There are frozen dumplings, condiments, and things you never thought of, like frozen tubs of Vietnamese beef broth base for pho. There is also a solid Asian vegetable section with a wide variety of greens, mushrooms, and tropical fruits. I was happy to see favorites of mine, like pea tips, dragon fruit, and fresh lychee.

The Asia Mall is not just a supermarket; there are two Vietnamese restaurants; one specializing in sandwiches and the other noodles; a Thai restaurant with no menu on display, and of all things, a Middle Eastern grocery with trays of classic pastries.

If you must choose between the Asia Mall and those Vietnamese markets in Philadelphia, I suggest going for the Asia Mall. It is right by an interstate and can be reached easily from a large swath of the state. You can come here, buy a case of instant ramen, a whole fresh catfish, have a meatball bahn mi sandwich, some curry, a bowl of noodle soup, and finish it off with a nice slice of baklava. It is a real Southeast Asian journey without going into the big city.

The sign outside welcoming you to the Asia Mall

THE BELLEVILLE
LIVESTOCK AUCTION

MIFFLIN COUNTY
26 SALE BARN LN., BELLEVILLE, PA 17004;
(717) 935-2146

When I saw people seriously bidding on pecan pies at the weekly Belleville livestock auction, I was left scratching my head. These were the same pies they could have bought at market tables just a few steps away and in fact, they were going for about the same price.

I thought that visiting the livestock auction—which was also something of a flea market and farmers' market—was a good idea. After all, there was a crowd, buggies from three different Amish sects, and an awful lot of tables filled with every sort of stuff. There was produce, but it looked kind of sad. Shoppers were carefully examining the pea pods trying to figure out if they were meant to be eaten whole like Asian snow peas or shelled like English peas. They were too brown to think about and so were the little heads of broccoli sitting right next to them.

If your whole experience with the Amish is in Lancaster County, you may think that produce is the highlight of Amish food culture. It may be for us outsiders, but for the Amish themselves, there is a whole world of surplus groceries—boxes of cereal and bottles of ketchup for absurdly low prices. They were as much a part of the event as the vegetables and those boxes and bottles were subjected to some serious attention.

As for the baked goods, what are you supposed to do when you see so much of what you have already seen so much of? Yes, they have more, it is just that if you have seen two hundred whoopie pies at another market and there are five hundred at Belleville, so what?

The parking lot is a show of its own. It is one of the few places you can see the white buggies of the Nebraska Amish, perhaps the strictest of all of Pennsylvania's plain peoples. Note that they have no windscreen, and the one vehicle light is a gas lantern. Then check out the guys, they wear their pants with only one suspender. Could this be because two would be an extravagance?

There were also yellow buggies. These belong to another strict sect, the Byler Amish. Like the other Amish here, austere expressions that speak to a life of modesty and sacrifice mark their faces. They are there buying and selling quarts of habanero peppers, Snickers bars by the pound, and the sorts of hardware items you thought had not been sold in a hundred years. (Ax handles for example.) Of course, black sneakers were offered in every size.

The non-Amish were worth mentioning too. Camouflage pants, shirts, and jackets were the style. Nobody looked like they had a job with a dress code. No, slacks, no scrubs, certainly no suits or the sorts of fashion items you would buy at suburban malls. A surprising number smoked. Table after table sold guns, the smoke of their cigarettes a parody of the smoke their weapons may make. Gun stands were always manned by the sorts of grizzled, old guys who scared the pants off city-dwellers. I greeted one and he flashed a big smile. He asked me if I hunt. I bluffed. "Not this year." I did not hunt any other year either but left that detail unsaid.

The Big Valley is the Amish country of dreams. Even a cursory visit makes you realize that here, Amish is not a way of dressing, it is a way of living—a very deep and demanding way of living. Once you are done with the market, take a drive around the countryside. In season, you will find roadside stands and "country" shops selling quality local foods at reasonable prices. For the price of a head of cauliflower, you can have a chance at conversation with one of the locals.

Think of The Big Valley as what Lancaster County was like sixty years ago—minus the buffet restaurants. The green fields, grazing cattle, and the feeling of stark emptiness that is in the space where the corn ends and the sky begins remind you of what the vastness of American agriculture was like before all those convenience stores, subdivisions, and strip malls were built.

Standing in the presence of Nebraska and Byler Amish, you know you can never bridge the gap that generations of piety and separatism have created. On the following Sunday, or the one after, their image will haunt you. You will know that they are in a three-hour service in Old German and still not convinced that salvation is at hand. The worship practices of the Lancaster County Amish are no less intense to outsiders, it is just that in Lancaster, local Amish can end the Sabbath with a trip to Target or a cup of coffee at Starbucks, something the residents of Big Valley cannot do. It is a very long trip to the nearest chain store—even in a car. This isolation surely contributes to the strength of their faith.

There is a very demanding relationship with God.

BENNER'S BUTCHER SHOPPE

JUNIATA COUNTY
56 PLATT HOLLOW RD., THOMPSONTOWN, PA 17094;
(717) 535-5313

Benner's Butcher Shoppe has been in the quiet village of Thompson-town so long that nobody there could remember when it opened. Look for the sign that shows a cheerful butcher at his block. There, you will find a shop selling locally produced beef and pork to people from both near and far. It is the sort of place you would be happy to have in your neighborhood, and also worth a stop for any meat lover driving between State College and Harrisburg.

Benner's Butcher Shoppe in Thompsontown

Benner's is the perfect modern ideal of meat. There are no hipster trappings, no fancy condiments, and really . . . no fancy anything. Just cement floors, white walls, and coolers filled with beef and pork. Benner's sources its cattle from nearby farms and then sells the meat in a brightly lit store attached to a barn. When we talk about getting our food from the source, this is what we mean. Here, cornfields come right up to the edge of the parking lot.

After all that pastoral simplicity outdoors, it feels almost industrial in the store. I felt a bit relieved to see this. Meat cutting is not just a business; it is a science, a craft, and a discipline too. When you see how bright and clean it is, you get a shot of confidence in the product and by this standard, Benner's sparkled.

There is some real cured pork artistry here. Check out the Hungarian bacon with intense paprika seasoning. It is right alongside rows of sausages that range from

Foods to Look For: Whoopie Pies

If you spend any time in Pennsylvania Dutch County, you will come to recognize whoopie pies. They are a sort of sandwich of two crumbly cake layers with a thick smear of sugar cream in between. There is a standard chocolate version and dozens of variations—everything from oatmeal raisin to pumpkin red velvet.

Is it a cookie or a cake? It is called a "pie," but it surely is not anything like other pies. There is no crust or liquid filling and it does not even come in a pie tin. Nobody agrees about any of this stuff and it seems like people become whoopie pie experts just so they can argue. And boy do they. . . besides what they are, there are also debates about where they originated. Both Pennsylvania and Maine claim to be the birthplace and nobody can present enough clear evidence to discredit the other.

Further confusing the issue is the fact that when we first saw mentions in New England, they were called "Amish whoopie pies." This was during an era when the Amish population of New England was zero. And all this happened long before "Amish Country" became a tourist destination.

Before you buy yourself a pie, you will have to think carefully. Should it be the classic chocolate with cream filling or something off-the-wall? Pumpkin spice mint? Red velvet? Oatmeal? All are possibilities. Nobody can try them all in a day or a week, so I will share a secret with you; the colors and flavors may be different, but the experience is the same.

Stop at a rural stand or shop, especially if it is miles from anywhere and staffed by a classic farm family. All over Pennsylvania, small vendors will have a table covered with freshly harvested fruits and vegetables with a few whoopie pies on a plate in one corner. They are always a find and

A classic whoopie pie I had to take a bite first!

taking one along with a much bigger haul of summer greens and ripe tomatoes is a treat.

Whoopie pies come in so many wonderful varieties.

At mud sales, family days, or other Amish events, you can find something of a whoopie pie paradise with big trays covered with them and crowds struggling to make their choices. In either case, the sparkle of their plastic wrap covering will tell you what is there from a hundred yards away. The unique whoopie shape glistens in the light.

Grab some coffee from the nearest convenience store and unwrap your chosen pie. The sweetness will embrace you with a rural Pennsylvania gastronomic hug. Savor it slowly, make up your own mind about the different varieties, and know it as a local treat—something to reward you if you've done well or soothe you if you haven't. It is easy to get carried away.

Hungarian flavored bacon from Benner's

Italian to bratwurst. They make their own bolognas and hams here—it is Pennsylvania after all—and despite being a good distance from Dutch Country, they make their own scrapple (see p. 172) too.

When it comes to fresh meat, beef is the star of the show. I studied the New York strip and Delmonico steaks and then wound up buying a huge chuck roast. I thought I would cut it up, make some into a Thai red curry, and freeze the rest. Then I bought bacon, pork loin, pork chops, and a few other things too. I had drifted into a state of meat hypnosis, and when I snapped back to attention, I was not sure it could all fit in my tiny, urban home freezer.

Meat had become both dream and mission.

Back home, there was serious cooking to be done! My beef chuck was about three pounds, perfectly trimmed, and beautifully marbled. I wound up breaking it down into pieces. Some became that curry and what was left over will await a day when I cannot make the long drive to a small-town butcher and want a meal with the sort of substance that beef delivers. I do not buy meat like this very often, but I am pleased on the days that I do.

BETO'S PIZZA AND RESTAURANT

ALLEGHENY COUNTY
1473 BANKSVILLE RD., PITTSBURGH, PA 15216;
BETOSORIGINALPIZZA.COM; (412) 561-0121

Beto's is a small building stuck between a steep, wooded slope and a four-lane highway. Standing in the parking lot, you would think you were deep in West Virginia, you are not though. This is the city of Pittsburgh—okay, a part of the city where deer roam freely, but still less than four miles from downtown.

Beto's sells its pizza as cuts and trays, putting it in the Pennsylvania coal country tradition. That is about all it does to conform to modern pizza culture—Pennsylvania, American, Italian, global, or otherwise. What is the difference? Beto's serves its pizza with the cheese uncooked. At Beto's your cuts and trays come with heaps of provolone cheese shreds—I know that you know that provolone is not even supposed to go on pizza. Beto's does not care.

That provolone is served in fat shreds and whatever you and I may think; the Beto's team sees that cheese as a scraggly heap of dairy-based beauty. It sits on top of the cuts like a crown and they throw it on the salads too. I liked this. Because so many restaurants serve their pizza with cheese that is greasy or burnt, this is as much a relief as it is a culinary twist.

It is the same with the toppings. Some are precooked, and all just sit there, mingled with the cheese shreds. Were you the sort that ate mushrooms straight from the can? Then come here! A bunch of them add a magic that does not exist when they are blast-cooked in a pool of melted cheese. Even more compelling are the anchovies—whole fillets that are almost as big as sardines. If you like them, you will come to love them here.

The raw shreds are so unique that you have to wonder why nobody's copied them. Actually, they are unusual in Pittsburgh, but true pizza experts would recognize the cuts here as perfect examples of the "Ohio Valley" style of pizza making. Sometimes it is called "Steubenville Style" after the town forty miles to the west that first offered it. In either case, it means pizza roughly like what Beto's serves.

Experts on the genre assert that the cheese available to Ohio Valley pizza makers back in the forties and fifties burned too easily

A distinctive piece of Beto's pizza, called a "cut" in this part of the world

and this recipe was created to overcome it. It worked. Not only did it work, but it also created its own set of fans.

Was Beto a person? Nobody says anything. This is obviously one man's vision of how a re-invented, re-imagined pizza may be, but nobody's talking. I guess he could have some association with Steubenville, possibly. There appears to be a professional photo of a man with a dough mixer circa the mid-sixties on the wall. You will not find a caption though, and the staff offers no explanation.

What should you do? I am not so sure. Beto's is too strange to allow anybody who has eaten there to leave without forming a strong opinion. If your pizza dream has steamy hot strings of melted mozzarella, you will be keenly disappointed—at least once the shock wears off. The rest of us will ask if those shredded, almost hairy, cuts are anything like any other pizza.

Only at a theoretical level.

It may be easier to deal with if they did not call it pizza. Of course, that opens a Pandora's Box of its own—is there a definition of pizza that includes raw cheese? Groups that define pizza almost always do so to promote methods and ingredients from Naples, in the Italian Deep South. That means fast cooking of dough, sauce, and mozzarella cheese under very high heat—unless there is something from the ocean in the topping—then there is no cheese at all. None of this happens at Beto's. It is its own thing, no matter what they call it.

BIG ELK GARLIC FARM

CHESTER COUNTY
523 PUSEY MILL RD., LINCOLN UNIVERSITY, PA 19352;
BIGELKGARLICFARM.COM; (484) 880-9204

Somebody has to farm garlic in Pennsylvania, and one of the most legendary growers is Frank Weakland, the owner, farmer, and fanatic behind Big Elk Garlic Farm.

It did not take more than a few minutes of conversation for me to realize that I was in the presence of a true garlic lover. A man who was lucky enough to find his calling and smart enough to be able to follow through and succeed. When I asked Frank why he chose garlic, he answered with, ". . . if you plant corn and it does not come up good, you are going to lose . . . but with garlic you will still make money."

His description of how he discovered it was equally pragmatic—back in 1999, he saw an ad in a magazine that suggested he grow "gourmet" garlic and ordered ten pounds of seed. There were some big differences between the corn and soybeans he was growing then and the garlic he was starting to plant. Garlic was manual; the big-name crops all used expensive machinery and took up vast acreage. Garlic was compact. You did not have to use much land to get a good crop. As the land he rented to farm continued to sprout suburban condos, and as the cost of mechanized farming went up, garlic beckoned.

Practical so far, right? There had to be a secret lurking in the background somewhere and when Frank said, "I eat garlic with my food and food with my garlic," I knew I had discovered the underlying truth—Frank was a total garlic fanatic. I asked if he was a fan of the intensely flavored Mexican restaurants of Kennett Square (see p. 129), a few short miles from his home. "No," he told me. "They do not use enough garlic."

I took a deep breath. Okay . . . if he were an accountant, I would say he was a bit nuts, he was a farmer though, and smart enough to find the pathway that allowed him to immerse himself in this single, potent food. There was no hiding behind a day job here! He loved garlic and it loved him back. It earned him a living, provided for his family, and was delicious too.

Garlic is a food superstar. It defines the taste of dozens of cuisines, it is a nutritional powerhouse, and it appears to have medicinal properties. You can be sympathetic, or even jealous of a guy like Frank who has channeled his passion and found a career.

When it comes to garlic types, German White is the variety of choice here. It is hardneck garlic—the kind with the long stem and easy-to-separate cloves—and has a slightly sweet and spicy flavor. I asked Frank if it resisted burning. I have noticed that so much garlic sold today burns too quickly, but he did not think that had anything to do with variety. He suspected that garlic cured artificially was too dry to cook with properly.

I had never even thought about this! It is not only the variety, but garlic also has to be cured and dried after it is picked and before it takes on the familiar form of bunched cloves. The curing method used affects flavor. Garlic that is dried naturally in fresh air will have a deeper and more complex taste. Artificially dried garlic will be weaker—although not milder—and a bit more bitter too.

There is another secret—a properly planted and well-tended acre and a half of quality garlic is more profitable than 350 acres of corn and soybeans. There are a zillion factors in that equation, less property tax, less equipment, less competition, more skill, and far higher commodity prices. And as Frank reminded me, "animals do not bother garlic . . . I am thankful that I have garlic, it is an equalizer, it allows me to pay my bills with a small bit of land." For one farmer, garlic is life.

BIRD-IN-HAN

LANCAS
2805 OLD PHILADELPHIA PI
(717) 76

When you visit the Amish, you get th ferently. You see them traveling by hor tinct outfits, and speaking their own la may well conclude that they have uniqu may make a few Pennsylvania Dutch pies a se, Amish food is basically American food. One ferent is that slow transportation prevents regular trip. Ig retail chains on main highways.

When the supermarket is too far, Amish people turn to their own convenience stores. Peppered through most of the large Amish settlements, you'll find the sorts of basic foods that large American farm families would need . . . and not much else. The only luxury is candy and the candy these shops sell is not all that luxurious.

As with all things Amish, the tone is modest. Look for flours, cereals, and beans in plastic bags and spices and flavorings in plastic tubs. It is telling that people who call themselves "plain" buy their staple foods in plain packaging. Even the candy is in plain plastic bags.

If you happen to be an Amish farmer, Bird-In-Hand Farm Supply is your mega-store. It has a wide selection of equine supplies, housewares that do not have to be plugged in, and in the back and behind a plastic curtain, groceries. Look for those plastic bags and containers. They are out in full force.

There is a dairy case worth checking out too. Big jugs of yellow-tinged raw milk are sold at low prices. If you are a raw milk fan, you already know about the place, but other people should be buying here too. Home cooks who make milk-based dishes and cheeses will discover that starting with quality raw milk will deliver flavors that are more vivid.

Make a point of looking for Phillips Lancaster Farmer Cheese. It is nothing like the Eastern European farmer cheese you find in the big cities, indeed, it is closer to mass-market, American provolone. This cheese embodies the Amish spirit perfectly. It is modest, flavorful, and inexpensive. It is cheese with a message—wholesome food that is straight off the farm should be for anybody; not just the rich.

Buggies parked in front of Bird-In-Hand Farm Supply, an Amish bulk food and housewares store in the heart of Lancaster County

Do not look for much in the way of meat or produce. You may find a commercial bologna or bushel of apples, not more though. The rural farmer customers here buy their meat a whole animal at a time and get most of their fresh produce from their own gardens. You will find big bags of frozen vegetables though; they are a winter staple. Instead, dry goods are the stars, big sacks of flour and oats, seasonings, and bulk packs of instant mixes. Imagine what you can and cannot make on your small farm to get a sense of what is offered.

One warning—check labels carefully. You will find some items that were bought retail at the big warehouse stores, marked up, and re-sold. These products may be appealing to the Amish, but not to those of us who can stop off at the same discount stores on our way home.

BRADDOCK COMMUNITY OVEN

ALLEGHENY COUNTY
1335 BRADDOCK AVE., BRADDOCK, PA 15104;
BRADDOCKCOMMUNITYOVEN.COM

The town of Braddock is a mixed signals sort of place. It is about eight or nine miles southeast of Pittsburgh and known for its poverty and decay. It is also a place where people do not give up. Former Mayor John Fetterman (yes, the big guy who made his way to Harrisburg) said of the place, "Reinvention is the only option." On the national stage, its only claim to fame is as a location for apocalyptic movies—no place in Pennsylvania looks worse in the eyes of Hollywood.

So many of its abandoned industrial buildings have become vacant that it has started to attract an outdoor, urban farming scene. On lots that once held factories and shops, you will now find a multi-acre farm and a hand-built, outdoor bread oven.

Community ovens are a favorite topic for food activists and are absolutely wonderful to contemplate. Here's the theory; at a given time, the oven manager would fire it up, local people would gather with their dough and form strong community bonds while baking high-quality breads.

In practice, it almost never works. Ovens like these take hours to fire up and huge amounts of wood to keep them going. Getting members who can make enough dough to justify doing it in the first place and then figuring out a time when enough of them can be ready to bake are tasks that are almost impossible to surmount. Somehow, Braddock pulls it off.

It works in Braddock for the strangest of reasons; almost nobody is interested enough to argue. If the place were filled with passionate bakers, they would be quarreling over the right time to start the fire and endlessly debating whether members should be banned for not using organic flour.

So, what is this real village oven with a five-by-seven-foot hearth doing in an almost-abandoned steel mill town? The present oven takes the place of a much smaller one built back in 2008. It was intended as something that local people could use and as it turned out, nobody really knew how. Poorly constructed and without regular care, it soon needed replacing. That is where Shauna Kearns came in.

She was a graduate student from Toronto who knew her community ovens backward and forward. Talking to her, you would think that Canada's biggest city was known more for its ovens than its huge tower or vast array of underground shopping malls. She took one look at the site and was hooked. With the title of "Co-Facilitator," she turned things around.

Soon, there was a new oven and a new program to go with it. Not serious bakers sharing, no. Instead, Shauna created a schedule of events around the times the oven would be fired up. Yes, there were days when bread was baked, and there were pizza nights too. For those, they set up tables of dough, sauce, and toppings that were formed and baked by folks from surrounding blocks. International nights followed. With these, the oven was the setting for meals representing cuisines from all over the planet. People started coming. First a few, then sixty or eighty. Many were neighbors, but the rest were from every corner of Pittsburgh.

There was some attempt at commercial use—a local restaurant sold pizzas and drinks on the site for a short while, but it was still the Braddock Community Oven. And Braddock remained a place that has resisted gentrification with vigor. This is where friends shared a meal on the rubble of what was once the backbone of industrial America. Turning it into a fancy place would mean hiding an awful lot of history.

Today, there is still no baker at Braddock, Shauna "facilitates," setting the dates for the events, finding guest cook/hosts for the international nights, and making sure the ingredients are all there when the time is right. At those moments, the oven is for the community . . . it is the community . . . and maybe it is even more.

BRIDGE STREET CHOCOLATES

CHESTER COUNTY
158 BRIDGE ST., PHOENIXVILLE, PA 19460;
BRIDGESTREETCHOCOLATES.COM; (610) 935-8100

Bridge Street Chocolates in Phoenixville is the sort of place that would not have survived in the decaying downtowns of the past. It has been in business for eight years, long enough to have seen Phoenixville change. In a town like this, that makes it an anchor business. Its offerings are better than what you can find in the supermarket and quite a bit cheaper than what you will see at shops that work with single-origin products.

The woman behind the counter told me that there were more than fifty different kinds of chocolate for sale that day. It was a good variety—big enough to keep you busy trying to decide and small enough not to confuse you. Also appealing was the craft going on behind the counter—the sight of the chocolatier at work and the rhythmic tapping sound of air bubbles being driven out of the chocolate.

Back home, I started my tasting with the sea salt drops. For some reason, I expected them to be the size of the chocolate chips you find in cookies. They were not though, instead, each was almost as big as a penny. The drops were mostly smooth but with the coarseness

Seasoned chocolate barks from Bridge Street Chocolates in Phoenixville

of a few salt crystals on the surface. I thought the salted drops were very clever. Not really sweet, but the salt amplifying what little bit of sweetness was there. Salted sweets can sometimes be baffling, but these made sense.

I also tried the *aleppo* pepper chocolate bark. I confess to being drawn to its vivid red specks of pepper and was curious to try something with a color I had never seen in a chocolate before. The tiny bit of heat offered a nice finish after the initial intensity wore off. It was much more enjoyable than the chile-infused stuff I had at the Chile Pepper Food Festival at Bowers a few months earlier (see p. 45) and in my opinion, a good choice for spice lovers.

There were also chocolate graham crackers, pretzels, salt and pepper bark, and almond bark. All had the same distinct flavor signature that comes with custom blended chocolate. It was obviously better than what I was used to. Their chocolate has less sugar than milk chocolate, so Bridge Street's has to use better raw materials. That includes Callebaut and Van Leer (No relation to the yodeling seventies rock star.) products.

It all led to a strange paradox. All those nuts and salts and spices do nothing if the chocolate underneath is not great, and if it is, they are nothing more than a distraction. The plain chocolate bars here are enough. The most delicious flavor of chocolate is chocolate.

BROAD STREET MARKET

DAUPHIN COUNTY
1233 N. 3RD ST., HARRISBURG, PA 17102;
BROADSTREETMARKET.ORG; (717) 236-7923

There are an awful lot of vendors at the Broad Street Market in Harrisburg. Get a cheesesteak, a burger, pierogies, some tacos, Korean tofu soup, jerk chicken, barbecue, or African goat soup . . . actually you can get Jamaican goat soup and African goat soup from adjoining stands. And then there is wine, a brewery, and a distillery too.

If there were a place like this in Manhattan, it would be a global destination. Correct me if I am wrong, but is not there always talk of opening a place like this there? It too would have food from all those countries and prices that were at least double what they charge here.

And of course, people who live a few short miles from Harrisburg would travel for hours to get the same thing in the Big Apple. I have seen it all happen before.

These are good reasons to go—it is a food court and market in an urban area not far from the state capitol—and the variety of vendors seemed like a sort of magnet for immigrant food enthusiasts. Then there is another and even more practical boast: This is the largest urban market in the state that offers free parking. Come early and you will find a spot right outside. It does not matter that much

The big outdoor sign announcing the entrance to the Broad Street Market in Harrisburg

though; the Broad Street Market is more about prepared food than shopping. This is the place to go if you want to taste Greek, Korean, Polish, and African in a single afternoon.

I hesitated a bit before I visited. It was not anything about what or where it was, instead, it was about its "oldest market" claim. The

A bowl of that Korean favorite, kimchee jjigae, from a vendor at the Broad Street Market in Harrisburg

Broad Street Market is not the only one in Pennsylvania that says it is the "oldest." All too many of these market house buildings boast about their age in one way or another and I did not want to become some sort of historical detective.

The market buildings may have been here all that time, but I do not think they have offered the huge variety of cooked foods they do now. When you walk the two aisles, about the only things that look like they may have had forty years ago are the butchers with their roasts, sausages, and ground beef and produce vendors with baskets of apples, turnips, and beets.

It is all divided between two buildings. The one under the big sign is called the "Stone Building" and the other behind it is the "Brick Building." In between are platforms where seasonal vendors can sell outdoors in good weather. Sadly, I missed this. I have always wound up visiting in the dead of winter.

Luckily, no matter how cold it is outside, there is warm food waiting. I started my visit to the Stone Building with a solid bowl of the Korean tofu soup called Kimchi Jjigae. It was spicy, sour, and filled with enough different textures to keep you studying your bowl for a while. The presence of tofu, mussels, scallions, and poached egg kept me guessing. Tofu and egg were similar, mussels were very different, and the pungent broth pressured them all into cooperating.

If that is not your favorite, try the Greek salad directly opposite. Actually, there were a couple of salads listed by their Greek names. I am no linguist, but I spotted *horiatiki* on a chalkboard. It would have to wait for my next visit. If you keep walking toward the back and past the goat soups, you will find an almost-hidden cheesesteak stand and a doorway leading outside. The Brick building will be directly in front of you. At least that is what other people call it. I think of it as the "Doughnut Building." It is in this hall that the notion of hipster vs Amish—briefly an internet meme, comes to life.

Doughnuts tell the story, Fisher's Bakery makes them in the classic Pennsylvania Dutch style and a few steps away, Evenella Donut Shop takes the "gourmet" route, with fancier toppings and a creative flair that is either appealing or intimidating depending on which side of the divide you are on. Could you even decide? I wound up eating both and getting so full that I could not taste half the things I had come to try. (And some of those were other doughnuts.)

Like the Reading Terminal Market (see p. 167), Broad Street is more of a place to eat than to shop, you can shop though. There are those butchers, produce in season, and an Amish style bulk foods vendor. What makes this an eating rather than shopping destination seems to be its proximity to jobs. On a nice day, huge numbers of commuting workers can stroll on down from the state capitol and buy a much better meal than what is normally available.

Yes, markets all over the state are being re-invented as food courts, but at least they are food courts that represent the neighborhood. You can walk into the Broad Street Market and do just what you could 150 years ago—buy the food local people themselves eat. The format may have changed, but the idea is still the same.

BUCKWHEAT CAKES AT THE UNITYVILLE FIRE COMPANY

LYCOMING COUNTY
6187 STATE ROUTE 42, UNITYVILLE, PA 17774;
(570) 458-4437

It was time for a firehouse breakfast, traditionally held the weekend following Thanksgiving, so, in the freezing cold dead of night, I dragged myself out of bed and set my GPS for the town of Unityville, deep in the Endless Mountains. Knowing there were buckwheat cakes on the menu, I was so excited that I drove three hours without a doughnut. It was a rare chance to eat what was once one of Pennsylvania's most iconic regional foods.

An early kind of pancake, buckwheat cakes were made by mixing water, buckwheat flour, and live sourdough starter: wheat flour, sugar, milk, and eggs were all optional. Most of the time it was just grain, water, and leavening. That sourdough gave them a distinct and unique vinegar tang.

Roadside restaurants used to make them and kept their own sourdough starters as a matter of course. Not anymore—the last cafe serving sourdough buckwheat cakes finally closed without fanfare.

The classic platter of buckwheat cakes, scrapple, and home fries from the long-closed Brass Pelican Restaurant outside Benton

The crowd at a buckwheat cake breakfast in Unityville

Local markets still sell buckwheat flour, although most of the time, baking powder takes the place of sourdough.

The firemen were offering "all you can eat buckwheat cakes (not sour), the best country store sausage you will ever eat, home-made sausage gravy, baked beans, fried potatoes, Unityville Fire Co's famous pickled cabbage, coffee, punch, milk and hot tea." They also promised that, "No one goes home hungry." I started worrying. I could fill up anywhere. I craved the delicious.

Depending on your mood, Unityville can look like a scene from some rural American novel or horror movie. There at a crossroads, was a market, a cemetery, a few wood and stone homes, and a cement firehouse located in the middle of rolling farm country. Zombies, guitar-strumming country singers, warmly remembered grannies, or top-secret military projects could all appear at any moment. It could have been home to the stories that inspired *Deliverance, Rebecca of Sunnybrook Farm, The Last House on the Left,* or *Andy of Mayberry.*

Inside the firehouse, there were rows of picnic tables filled with people eating. I bought a ticket for eight bucks and walked towardthe dining area. It was rural Pennsylvania personified. Folks seemed to be in uniform. Everybody, from toddlers to the elderly wore some com-bination of printed tee shirts, jeans, cotton sweats, and fleece. The whole room was completely machine washable.

Sausage patties at the Unityville buckwheat cake breakfast Without my glasses on, I have mistaken them for pancakes

At the table, some people finished up while others were being seated. Platters were placed in the middle and refilled as they emptied. When I began, there was sausage, gravy, and cabbage—enough to get a good start. The buckwheat cakes themselves were not brought to my table for a few more minutes. They certainly were not sour. Mine were sort of splatter-shaped, as thin as French crepes; nutty, a little oily from the grill, and even had bits of crunch.

Seated there, the rest of the diners barely interrupted their discussions of other people's diseases to slather margarine, syrup, sawmill gravy, and beans over their cakes. I expected them to look wholesome and healthy—perhaps like perfect fried discs of multigrain bread—and they did not.

The firemen were right; there was nothing sour at all. Even the pickled cabbage, a nice winter vegetable touch, was sweeter than tart. Would sourdough have made them better? In a purely theoretical sense, yes. Is there any way that a bunch of volunteer firemen could have cultured enough sourdough for five thousand portions? Not that I could imagine.

I was bothered by what was lost. Sour, pungent, vivid. All too often today, we hardly notice the taste of foods as they slide down our throats. What are we missing? Sourdough in the cakes, molasses in the beans, porky saltiness in the sausage and gravy, and a whole different sort of fermentation in the cabbage. A hundred years ago, the weakest thing would be the coffee. Nonetheless, it was all really good—a solid firehouse meal.

Pennsylvanians have always loved buckwheat. We eat it in scrapple (see p. 172), pancakes, and in immigrant dishes like kasha and soba. Firehouse breakfasts may not be the most perfect of culinary historical re-creations, but without those old roadside cafes, they are our last link to this local, traditional food. We owe them our respect and our patronage too.

BUFFALO VALLEY PRODUCE AUCTION

UNION COUNTY
22 VIOLET RD., MIFFLINBURG, PA 17844;
BUFFALOVALLEYPRODUCE.COM; (570) 966-1151

JUNIATA PRODUCE AUCTION

JUNIATA COUNTY
1055 RED ROCK RD., MIFFLINTOWN, PA 17059; (717) 463-2484
AUCTION DAYS AND TIMES ARE SUBJECT TO CHANGE.

Very few places in the Pennsylvania food world will leave you scratching your head the way the Buffalo Valley Produce Auction does. This seemingly remote spot—miles from the nearest gas pump and surrounded by cornfields—is a buzzing hub of the fruit and vegetable trade.

On market days, you will find rows of whatever is currently being harvested in the eastern United States. Tomatoes, peppers, peaches, apples, pumpkins, and more find their way to these open concrete and steel sheds where wholesale buyers study the lots as if they were looking for buried treasure.

You can tell the sellers know they are facing important buyers. Nothing is in heaps. Everything is packed perfectly—the management sells packaging materials and offers instructions in order to make sure everything looks its best—even the beets were neatly boxed.

A full day at the Buffalo Valley Produce Auction

A hand-lettered sign welcoming you to the Juniata Produce Auction in Mifflintown

All this made me ask how I was supposed to view it. Was it an urban outpost? A bit of country? Most of the sellers and many of the buyers were either Amish or Old Order Mennonite, but there were no buggies. Everything came and went by truck, some of them very big. And nobody batted an eyelash at the prospect of buying a few hundred watermelons.

There, in those aisles of neatly packed boxes, were three separate, simultaneous auctions, each with their own computer cart and demonstrator. While the auctioneers spat their banter into microphones, the demonstrators—Amish or Old Order Mennonite women—would hold up single pieces of whatever was being sold while gazing into the crowd with blank looks. Apparently, none had ever seen a television game show.

I found it impossible to distinguish between the auctions. The different bids and prices coming at once from three nearby speakers gave the place a stiff dose of the surreal. This was made even tougher by the use of the word "item" to mean a whole case. Indeed, at one point, I was mistakenly convinced that somebody just paid seventeen bucks for an eggplant.

The Buffalo Valley Produce Auction was certainly an important spot. People often talk about knowing where your food comes from and being there answers the question in a very literal sense. The farmers who grow it bring it in trucks parked right in front of you, and the markets that so many of us shop in take it away in other trucks with store logos on the sides.

Baffled by the confusion on the selling floor, I wandered over to a food truck staffed by a couple of Old Order Mennonite women. I asked if they would make me a scrapple sandwich (see p. 172). "We do not have any, Nobody's making it now" was the answer. I was not sure what she meant and wanted clarification. "People around here do not usually make it this time of year and we won't serve it unless it is made by somebody we know." The other guys waiting for their food nodded with enthusiasm. I was assured that this is where I would find the best scrapple anywhere, except during the summer.

Buffalo Valley is not the only produce auction in the area. The Juniata Produce Auction is thirty miles or so southwest. They may only be an hour of driving apart, but the psychological distance is best measured in light-years. Pull up to the auction shed here and watch as horse-drawn plows work the fields right next door.

If you are headed to Juniata, I do not recommend waiting to the last second before you go. In the moments before the market opens, the road out front is jammed with buggies and horse carts. Local farmers are picking until the

A big box of spaghetti squash right from the farm

last possible second and do not even split their crops into bushels and baskets until after they get there. This auction is so close to the land that many of the lots do not even come by motor vehicle.

"Meet the producer" is pretty much compulsory here. Look closely at a box of tomatoes and the person who grew them will almost certainly approach you. There is a flip side to this too. Ask anybody what

Pumpkins for sale at the Juniata Produce Auction in Mifflintown

they are doing and they will mark you as a hopelessly uninformed outsider. And this place is so remote that almost everybody new is an outsider. There is no introduction, no explanatory brochure, just an Amish guy who announces, "Okay! Bidding starts now!"

I was there on Labor Day and even then, there were no tourists. They had to sell on a holiday because it was peak harvest season. The market was filled with melons and pumpkins and they all had to be sold. Nothing could be worse than food rotting while retail customers a few hundred miles away wanted everything that was being offered. These small farmers could not risk the loss.

The modest scale calms things down. It is easy to see what is being sold and who is doing the bidding. The auction patter is still tough to understand, but at least the numbers are comprehensible. People here bid on fruits and vegetables by the pound or bushel. Winning bids are not secret either, they are written by hand on the tags that mark each lot.

It is tempting to suggest that you should visit Juniata if you are in the area, but who is ever in this area? Go anyway! Both it and the Buffalo Valley auctions will teach you a powerful lesson about the journey that fresh produce takes from farm to store.

CALLIE'S CANDY KITCHEN

MONROE COUNTY
1111 ROUTE 390, MOUNTAINHOME, PA 18342;
CALLIESCANDY.COM; (570) 595-2280

Callie's Candy Kitchen has been in the Poconos so long that it has a museum of its own history. It was started by Harry and Carol Callie way back in 1952. In those days it was in Bangor, a bit to the south and closer to Allentown and Bethlehem. By the early seventies though, they had moved to their present location in Mountainhome, just a bit north of Mount Pocono.

This is an area that is hard to define. It is got suburbia, outlet shopping, casinos, and even some industry. Each time you think you have a handle on the place, you discover something that makes you see it differently. No matter what your reason is for being here, Callie's is your go-to shop for candy.

What makes Callie's worth a visit is the way they tread the delicate line between popular and artisan. There are some quality truffles in the case in front and miniature soda pop cans filled with fizzy stuff too. It is not as serious as Shane's Confectionery in Philadelphia (see p. 186) and yet somehow, it is far more so than Mister Ed's (see p. 132). At Callie's Candy Kitchen, you can buy chocolate cigars for the kiddos;

Callie's Candy Kitchen from the outside

cashew brittle for a snack; themed, molded chocolate for a party; and those truffles for the people in your life who are a bit more serious about their chocolate.

Callie's has fun stuff scattered throughout the whole place. Some rooms are for classic candies, which is where you will find things like those fizzy cans and Tootsie Rolls. Another room holds serious snacks. It has a whole area with "barks"—sheets of flavored

Taken during the Covid epidemic, this statue in front of Callie's Candy Kitchen encourages proper mask wearing

and decorated chocolate that have been broken into large chips. Nearby are peanut and cashew nut brittles, they are the same shape as the barks and a whole different flavor experience. Almost in the same department are the chocolate-covered potato chips. These seem to be completely alien and totally perfect at the same time.

Then, on the far side of the place, baby shark and unicorn lollipops caught my eye, so did the circus "peanuts" and brilliantly colored bits of rock candy. Scattered throughout the store are pretzels, chocolate-covered of course, and yogurt covered too. With rods, nuggets, and twists, it is easy to lose track of the different sizes and shapes.

The chocolate truffle case is front and center. Here you will find the classics with some more modern items like chocolate-covered Oreos and graham crackers mixed in. These are not Pennsylvania's most sophisticated truffles, but they are a very good value.

Did I leave out the mints, licorice, hard candies, and popcorn? Maybe I did . . . you will still find them there though.

Finally, there is one room you have to see: the museum. There are copies of *Candy Making for Dummies*, photos of the Callies attending conferences and accepting awards, a couple of old enrobing machines of the sort that could evenly chocolate coat just about anything, and a collection of old rabbit and Santa molds. Look them over and you cannot help noticing that there is nothing silly or pretentious there. Harry and Carol always had good taste.

CAPUTO BROTHERS CREAMERY

YORK COUNTY
245 N. MAIN ST., SPRING GROVE, PA 17362;
CAPUTOBROTHERSCREAMERY.COM; (717) 739-1091

There is a seriousness to Caputo Brothers Creamery that you can feel as you walk through the door. It is all about cheese—Italian cheese. It is not in a place with a long tradition of Italian cookery and artisanship, but it is a perfect spot to make some very good, very authentic cheese. It all happens in their shop, a converted former car dealership in rural York County.

Caputo Brothers is Italian in a way that is really different than—for example—what is considered Italian in Pittston and Old Forge (see p. 144). We are talking about two different kinds of authentic. Those other places are Italian in the sense that local people work hard to preserve the traditions of Italian immigrants who came long ago. Caputo is Italian because they produce cheeses very similar to ones you will find in southern Italy today.

Come on in. Cheese shops that bring in products from all over the world will have vast selections and tough choices. Not here. The only cheese sold is cheese they make in this very building. You will find nine or ten choices in a small cooler off to one side.

In that case, you may find a provola of one sort or another, maybe a provolone, maybe a provola riserva. Of course, there is ricotta, it is the by-product of the mozzarella that is their biggest seller. You will not see mozzarella in the display case though, that is behind the counter where they make it. They are very fussy here.

Most importantly for me, Caputo Brothers is a stronghold of serious technique. You take this for granted at places like Valley Milkhouse (see p. 208) or Dove Song Dairy (see p. 60) but Italian style cheeses in America suffer from a century of shortcuts. For example, ricotta here is made from cultured whey, not from acidulated milk.

Maybe I should clarify—ricotta means "re-cooked" in Italian. The cheese is called that because it is made from whey that has been re-heated to extract that last bit of cheese from the liquid. This is great if you are already making mozzarella because you will have plenty of whey left over. Best of all, it gives a modest operation like Caputo Brothers two basic products right from the start.

I have to clarify something else too. The mozzarella and ricotta that Caputo Brothers makes comes from cow's milk. The deepest of Italian cheese fanatics will insist that at some official level, mozzarella has to be made from water buffalo milk. Sadly, there are not yet enough water buffalo in Pennsylvania to provide it.

Caputo does buy its milk straight from local farms—even if it is not from water buffaloes. The three thousand or so gallons of milk a week that they use is enough to keep at least a dairy farm or two in business. For small-scale cheese makers, this is a big question. Some, like Dove Song Dairy actually started making cheese as a way to use the milk produced on their farm. Others, like Caputo and Valley Milkhouse, buy their milk from local farmers. This creates an interesting symbiotic relationship. The farmers support the cheese and the cheese supports the farmers.

Back in the shop, I started picking out pieces of cheese to buy. They are all pre-cut and shrink-wrapped. There is not much retail traf-

A plastic tub of the ricotta from Caputo Brothers Creamery in York County

fic here and that is what they—and most Pennsylvania cheese producers—have to do in order to keep it reasonably fresh. Luckily, the packed wedges are tiny and priced by the ounce. I can take a couple, confident I can finish them before they dry out.

My visit was on a weekday afternoon and there was not much of a crowd. Caputo Brothers offers both cooking classes and themed meals though, and on those days, it will be packed. Reservations are absolutely required.

All serious cheese makers have to be in places that are at least a bit remote for consumers. What counts for them is proximity to cows, not customers. Keep that in mind while you are on your way. We modern shoppers think of cheese as something fancy, but that is not quite correct, cheese is a product of the land, the best requires a journey.

CHILE PEPPER FOOD FESTIVAL

BERKS COUNTY
WILLIAM DELONG PARK, 233 BOWERS RD., BOWERS, PA 19511;
PEPPERFESTIVAL.COM; (610) 682-7045

I felt a quick jolt of adrenaline when I started wandering the grounds of the Chile Pepper Food Festival in Bowers. I could tell that these were my people! Everybody united by their desire to eat something just a bit spicier than what is typically served in the Keystone State. Watching them all as they moved from booth to booth, I knew they were the ones who complained when their Sichuan meals were too bland. I could tell they did not flinch at the sight of *kimchee* or Indian pickles (although there were no vendors offering either of these chili-laden items).

Attendees at the Chile Pepper Food Festival were the sorts who did not boast. They would just walk into a roadside barbecue restaurant in Oklahoma or New Mexico, get the hottest dish and tell their friends how much they loved it instead of how spicy it was. In Thailand or Mexico, they would eat the street food with gusto. No gringo stories here.

A basket of orange Scotch Bonnet peppers at the Chile Pepper Food Festival in Bowers

Of course, there was a clue; when you see the spicy vegetable spelled "chile" instead of "chili," it is meant as a message to the dedicated. It screamed fiery seriousness and acted as a sort of secret password. It announces, "We're not those folks who spell the name of our beloved food normally, 'chile heads' are here! Do not be bashful."

Because there are so many food festivals like this one, it pays to work out a strategy before you go. Here is mine:

First priority: parking. Just do it! Do not cruise through the neighborhood; do not try to outsmart the local volunteers who know the story. Park where they tell you to and get your car off the streets and out of the way as quickly as possible. Ease of parking is the best reason to come early.

Second: I will call this "triage." What should you be looking for? What may be less important? What are the time wasters? I suggest you concentrate on the classics. A bowl of chili at a chili festival seems like a plan. Other traditionally spicy dishes make sense too. How about pulled pork or jerk chicken? Novelty items like chili-infused cookies or candies could well be good, but they come last. Fill yourself up with these things first and you will have wasted the opportunity to get the real stuff.

Third: budgeting. Think carefully about how much you are willing to spend before you part with a penny. Even if every one of those hot sauces is delicious, do you really want ten or fifteen of them in your kitchen? Do not spend so much on packages and bottles that you wind up missing the foods that make the festival special.

And fourth: You are there for the food. Have a real meal; something that reminds you that the food the festival celebrates is worth the trouble and trip. At Bowers, you could start with a bowl of chili of course, and then barbecue or jambalaya. I sought out spicy cuisines that I do not normally eat and wound up with a great Jamaican codfish fritter. It made the day.

Sated with a great bowl of chili and that codfish fritter, it was time to start tasting the novelties. I could see that nobody was following my advice; the lines were far longer at vendors of chili-infused candy or cookies than they were at the stands selling actual cooked meals. I joined them against my better judgment. Chili chocolate chip cookies and chili peanut brittle were fun and almost as good as they would have been had they left the chili out. These things are novelties for a reason.

Most of the crowd did not have much to say as they sampled the hot sauces, there were hundreds of them and if you do not do it on a regular basis, they all seem to taste the same. Listen a bit more carefully though and you will start recognizing the cognoscenti—people who know peppers by variety and view the experience as an esoteric equivalent of a wine tasting.

Heat, fruit, sour, sweet, and maybe overtones of chocolate or leather too. It is fascinating the way we describe flavors with other flavors. Poor chocolate! Everything has hints of chocolate! Wine, beer, and with this group of experts, hot sauce too. What do they say at chocolate tastings?

Something else has to be noted: There were far fewer products described with coarse language than there were years ago. The name

The real thing, Pennsylvania style A bowl of chili with shredded cheese at the Chile Pepper Food Festival in Bowers

of every hot sauce could be mentioned on broadcast television. You could read almost every description to your elderly aunts. I saw one sauce that described itself by saying something like, "We provide the heat; you provide the toilet paper." Years ago, this would have been the least of it, today, it seemed juvenile rather than shocking.

When we attend these festivals, we are nothing more than visitors. It is easy to name the things that are missing: Indian curries and pickles, Korean kimchee, Chinese infused oils, and African . . . well, African anything. I realized the only solution would be me becoming a vendor, so I kept these complaints to myself.

On my way out, I bought a cup of Thai iced coffee. I loved it in Bangkok and thought it may cool things down here too. I was right. It was a parting reminder that behind the novelties and glass bottles were some great cuisines.

CLOVER CREEK CHEESE CELLAR

BLAIR COUNTY
5161 CLOVER CREEK RD., WILLIAMSBURG, PA 16693;
CLOVERCREEKCHEESE.COM; (814) 515-9873

All too many Pennsylvania dairy farms are closing. Even though each one is different, their reasons are the same: low fluid milk prices. There is a kind of paradox though; as our dairy farms vanish, sales of fine cheeses are doing better than ever. For those of us who do not raise cows for a living, it is easy to ask why dairy farmers do not switch from fluid milk to cheese.

Making the switch is one of those things that is really easy to say, and incredibly difficult to do. Those European cheeses you see in the supermarket are produced by people who have perfected their skills over generations. This gives them a huge advantage. A newly minted dairy farmer in France or Italy can tap into the vast knowledge base held by their neighbors and relatives. They can easily find inexpensive equipment to get them going too.

Pennsylvania cheese makers have to start from scratch. Almost nobody has a neighbor or relative who can show them how, and even if they did, the equipment they would need costs a fortune. This is why so many cheese makers offer classes. The demand is huge and skills need to be shared.

That is the story at Clover Creek Cheese Cellar. When it got started, Dave Rice and his wife Terry did little more than milk cows. It did not pay the bills though, so they spent some time considering how they could add value. The first change was to grazing. They had quite a bit of land. Its slopes were too steep for mechanized crop farming, but the soil and the grass made for perfect pasture. The cows were happy too.

The valley Clover Creek sits in used to be a place where large quantities of fluid milk were put in metal containers and shipped to the big cities. Indeed, Dave found a milk shipment receipt dated 1910 while he was cleaning out the barn. Even a hundred years ago, the milk was the product itself. If it was going to be made into something else, that happened someplace else.

Grazing works out well. It is inexpensive, and cows in the pasture—doing what cows do—are great at controlling erosion. And besides, the cows love it. They wander up, find a nice patch of fresh grass, eat for a while, stroll to the bottom, find a nice flat spot, lie down, and digest. A good lifestyle by cow standards.

Learning to make aged, hard cheeses became their goal. Dave and Terry visited and studied with cheese artisans in Pennsylvania, Virginia, Ohio, Vermont, Tennessee, and Texas. Dave told me that while these farms varied in many different ways, all were willing to share. In fact, the learning never stopped, and thanks to a scholarship from Slow Food, they got to study the process in Argentina—an unusual move in this normally European-facing craft.

A wedge of Bruschedda, an herbed cheddar, from the Clover Creek Cheese Cellar

People who pay top dollar for hard cheeses are very different from bulk milk buyers though. Dave described the first time he had a truly demanding and serious customer. "She sniffed it, checked the texture by rolling it in her hand, and finally tasted our cheese. After a few minutes, she commented, 'This cheese was made in June while the cows were out on pasture.'"

She was correct and he was astounded. This is absolutely not the same as filling a tank truck with milk and getting a check in the mail.

Not everybody is that demanding. Dave told me about the time the process did not quite work out. "We also had a cheddar that did not cheddar, so we named it UNCheddar. One lady claimed it tasted just like the cheese her mother made in the old country."

Clover Creek is starting to thrive. They are now producing about twenty thousand pounds of cheese a year and their son has taken over the cellar. They have a daughter too and she studies agriculture in college. It has turned out to be a happy place for cows and people too.

CROSSROADS BAKE SHOP

BUCKS COUNTY
812 N. EASTON RD., DOYLESTOWN, PA 18902;
CROSSROADSBAKESHOP.COM; (215) 348-0828

The Crossroads Bake Shop is not at a real intersection. Instead, it sits at the crossroads of American and European baking. That means they are as enthusiastic about fruit pies as they are about baguettes. Marcia Durgin and her husband Paul Rizzo opened Crossroads almost three decades ago with the goal of excelling at both baking traditions. This has been no easy task. Maintaining the needed skills while training an ever-growing staff is more than just their jobs, it is their life's mission.

Their story began in Boston back when Paul and Marcia had just graduated college. They were trying to build careers in environmental science. Spending their days in sterile laboratories identifying toxins was not what they'd envisioned and it left them frustrated. After Marcia quit one lab job, she found herself working in a bakery. This was something she could pour herself into. Baking could pay her a wage, offer her a skill, and give her something to practice and perfect. Paul soon followed and they became both a couple and a team.

Marcia and Paul were ready for their own bakery and the only remaining question was where it was going to be. Boston was too expensive. They thought of Marcia's childhood town of Binghamton, New York, but it had a whole bunch of established and traditional bakeries. Then Paul's parents came though. They were living in Bucks County, Pennsylvania, and believed their baking would go over well there.

First, they tried selling breads and pies at a local farmers' market. Working out of a converted garage, they were a big hit. European breads and American pies were a perfect mix in an area that combines urban sophistication and a serious sense of history. The market closed for the season just before Thanksgiving and Marcia and Paul had a new shop open the following week.

They had big plans from the very beginning. Pies, croissants, sourdough loaves, and baguettes were on the menu and it soon grew in every direction. In homage to Binghamton, they baked salt-rising bread (see p. 177), and then flatbreads too. They had to stop making that salt-rising bread, but baguettes remain to this day.

Doylestown is not exactly the right place for bargain hunters, and yet, those baguettes are a great deal. For less than three bucks, you get a good-sized loaf. There are customers who have them as their one luxury. They may not be able to visit France, but a piece of authentically baked bread keeps their memories alive.

Today, Crossroads Bake Shop and its staff of more than twenty continue its mission of rustic baking. For Marcia, that means breads and pastries that are done as soon as they are out of the oven with minimal decorating and no cakes in the shape of elephants or super-heros. Even in this day of sculpted wedding cakes, nobody complains.

Thinking there were things that could be done better, Marcia told me that Crossroads once put out a suggestion box. The most popular suggestion? "Get rid of the suggestion box!" And the most common comment? "Do not change anything."

DAILY LOAF BAKERY

BERKS COUNTY
SEE DAILYLOAFBAKERY.COM TO FIND OUT
WHERE THE GOODS ARE SOLD.

What does bread taste like? Or maybe, what is bread supposed to taste like? Too many of us think bread is not supposed to have any flavor at all; that it is there only to support something else. If that is how you feel, you should know that Anna and Zane, the husband-and-wife team who run Daily Loaf Bakery in Hamburg disagree with you. They work really hard to produce bread with deep flavors. Since the only ingredients they use are flour, sourdough, salt, and water, it is no easy task . . . Actually, I am wrong here. Their sourdough is made only from flour and water.

Despite being bread fanatics, Anna and Zane had no real professional baking experience. This could well be for the better. If they'd worked in more typical Pennsylvania bakeries, they could have wound up using yeast, sugar, oil, or other additives—things that would never make it into the breads they bake today. Starting from scratch, they were able to scale up using only the most fanatical of techniques.

So, if there was no bakery lineage, how did Daily Loaf Bakery get started? Here is the scoop: Anna had baked some sourdough bread for a few friends and one loved it so much she began taking orders for future loaves without Anna's permission. That friend meant well. After all, there was no commercial bread like it and demand was high. Anna was not too happy to see the stack of orders, but she loved making bread. She fulfilled them and then made some more.

Producing bread this way gave Anna the chance to deep dive into her obsessions. It had to be sourdough with no commercial leavening, and whole grain too. She is so focused on whole grains that even her white bread has some whole wheat flour in it. Her baking technique became more like fermentation with batches of dough rising for as much as twenty hours to bring out the flavors and textures.

The place kept growing. A hundred loaves a week, two hundred, and now with Zane in the game full time, almost five hundred, and pastries too. They soon realized they were part of a bigger trend toward purer breads. Good bread, once the turf of small shops in France and Italy, was coming to America in the form of whole grain sourdough loaves. A bit different than European, but with the same spirit of excellence.

As food artisans get deeper into their craft, they tend to make friends along the way. For Daily Loaf Bakery, this means the way they source their ingredients. The flours they use come from small, family-owned mills and the grain from local farms, sources that are as serious as they are. In some cases—rye flour is a perfect example—they have to mill it themselves. If they used commercial rye flour, much of the flavor would be lost in storage, and besides, Anna would start worrying that it wouldn't be a complete, whole grain product.

Bread from Daily Loaf Bakery is not easy to come by. There is no handy shop, you can find their breads at a handful of farm stands and natural foods stores around Berks County and in season at the farmers' market in West Reading. You will find the details in the usual (online) places.

There is more to this than Anna and Zane's bread obsession. Those three ingredients; their flour, salt, and water have created a community and more than anything, those customers—the people who have morphed from customers to friends, are what keeps them going. Bread has connected them.

DEEP HOLLOW FOREST FARM

DAUPHIN COUNTY
2850 WHITE OAK RD., HALIFAX, PA 17032;
(717) 303-8327

Driving north through Harrisburg, you will notice the sudden change from fertile farmland to steep hills. There is the capitol, a tiny bit of suburbia, and then mountains wild enough to carry the Appalachian Trail. It is rugged country, almost the coal belt, and still home to at least a few logging operations. To most of us, this seems like wilderness. Yet historians and naturalists will find something else—land once cleared for subsistence farming and then abandoned. This is where you will find Deep Hollow Forest Farm, looking to all the world like yet one more tract of hilly, tree-covered scrub.

Before there was a Deep Hollow Forest Farm, there was a guy named Brian Scott, an RN with a job in Harrisburg, a quick mind, and a strong desire to do something agricultural with his new property. He'd been reading Wendell Berry and was inspired to think about what exactly the land was doing while nobody was disturbing it.

What was his land doing? Well, for one thing, it was filled with mushrooms. Brian started reading and quickly learned the basics. He wanted to be growing something in harmony with the land, and mushrooms—especially shiitake mushrooms—would do the job. Shiitake are a great variety to grow. They are filled with flavor and command a good price. Bedsides, most of the shiitake eaten in this country are imported in dried form and sold in Asian markets. Brian's would be fresh and local.

Even though we do not grow that much shiitake, mushroom cultivation is a big deal in Pennsylvania. Chester County alone is said to harvest more than a quarter of a billion pounds a year, almost half of America's total. They are mostly button mushrooms, criminis, and portobellos, folks there consider shiitake to be "exotic" and do not really take their cultivation seriously.

The mushroom farms in Chester County are not shady spots on the forest floor either. Instead, they are indoors with rigorous temperature and lighting controls that can be sterilized between crops. These structures, made from cinder blocks and with vault-like doors, are really better thought of as mushroom growing machines. They were not what Brian had in mind.

He soon discovered the process of growing on logs. It was simple in theory. You get some logs—pieces of oak that were too small for lumber and too big for firewood, drill holes in them, put some mushroom seeds in the holes, seal them up, and wait a year or two. It was not exactly that easy. The seeds, otherwise known as "spawn," were hard to get and harder to keep in the holes. Each mushroom farmer developed their own technique for fabricating the logs.

Outdoor mushroom farming requires serious scientific knowledge and great faith. It can be a year or more between the time you seed your first log and harvest a crop. While you are waiting, you do not get to see anything. No seedlings taking root, no clues at all, until one day you look out the window and those logs are filled with fruiting mushrooms. Then, a few years later, you see a thousand logs bearing fruit and realize you are a farmer in the forest.

Selling those harvested mushrooms was another story entirely. He had not yet grown enough to sell wholesale and most people in the area had never seen fresh shiitake before. He gradually built a following and soon markets around Harrisburg, and serious chefs, were taking as much as he could produce.

Shiitake are not the only mushrooms Brian grows. He has had good luck with hen-of-the-woods (called *maitake* by serious mushroom gourmets) and *nameko* too, although they have far shorter seasons. It all adds up. Logs that are a by-product of local wood cutting are combined with a crop that is not really so different than what was growing wild in the same place before he came. Thanks to his efforts, that bit of forest is producing something delicious.

DEITSCH ECK

BERKS COUNTY
87 PENN ST., LENHARTSVILLE, PA 19534;
THE-ECK.COM; (610) 562-8520

In my opinion, anytime would be the right time for scrapple (see p. 172), it is just that while the few remaining Pennsylvania Dutch restaurants may agree with this in theory, when push comes to shove, they are not open long enough or often enough to meet a reasonable definition of "anytime."

That is the case at the very Pennsylvania Dutch Deitsch Eck restaurant, right off I-78 a bit west of Allentown. Scrapple is a classic breakfast meat, but the Eck is not ever open for breakfast. All they offer is dinner on Wednesday through Sunday and Sunday lunch too. Your chance at real small-town Pennsylvania Dutch cooking is limited enough. These hours do not help.

Now that you've been warned, it is time to head on over. The place is larger than it looks from the outside. You can easily be seated in one of several dining rooms, all of which have Pennsylvania Dutch murals. Take a good look, not much remains of local folk culture and it wouldn't require more than a can of paint and a roller to lose these examples too.

There is no favorite dining room, any will do the job and none has a particularly beautiful view. Getting to the Eck takes you through some of the most pastoral farmland in the state but the restaurant windows face either parking or local buildings.

Give the menu a casual glance and you won't notice anything special. You really need to study it a bit. I already gave away the fact that they serve scrapple for dinner. You can get it as a scrapple appetizer, a main dish platter, or as part of a combo. On my last visit, I made my choice a combo platter of smoked sausage and scrapple. I upped the Pennsylvania Dutch theme with sides of the vegetable relish called "chow chow" and lettuce with hot bacon dressing.

Is there more to the menu? Yes. You can get typical roadside American meals; it is just that those Pennsylvania Dutch dishes buried among them are what make the place worth a visit. They begin with that scrapple, move on to smoked pork chops or sausage, and continue to the sides. On the day I was there, the sides I found were chow chow, potato filling, corn fritters, apple fritters, pepper cabbage, and

A bit of Pennsylvania Dutch meat heaven; a combo plate with a smoked sausage and scrapple at the Deitsch Eck in Lenhartsville

lettuce with hot bacon dressing. All resounding reminders of place, culture, and history. And then there was spaghetti; there to tell you that there were other immigrants to this area too.

If there is a word that describes the cooking here, it is "mild." The cuisine is mild and the kitchen is mild. The strongest flavors are sugar and vinegar. Dishes like chow chow and pepper cabbage will have both together. Sometimes this works and the food goes down with an easygoing comfort. There are also times when the mildness is overwhelming . . . when it feels like a bit of garlic or a few chili flakes would improve everything exponentially. Those are the moments when I curse the kitchen for sticking with tradition . . . when I resent them for the very reason I came in the first place.

There is pie for dessert—it is rural America after all. Apple crumb, egg custard, and shoofly were all choices recently. And with it, coffee so weak it looked like tea. My slice of egg custard pie was less sweet than the vegetable salad sides I had eaten moments before. Pennsylvania Dutch for real.

DIETRICH'S MEATS & COUNTRY STORE

BERKS COUNTY
660 OLD ROUTE 22, LENHARTSVILLE, PA 19534;
DIETRICHSMEATS.COM; (610) 756-6344

Before you even walk through the door at Dietrich's Meats, you will notice that the signs out front have the power to bring you happiness as a meat lover. The notice that they make their own knockwurst, bratwurst, and butcher bologna will get you smiling and the reminder that they render their own lard will elevate you to a state of true porcine joy.

With its billboards and right-off-the-interstate location, Dietrich's Meats does not seem like the most remote of destinations, and yet, almost nobody stops here. That is a shame, because this is one of the most complete butcher shops there is. You will find the steaks and roasts that you are more likely to associate with big-city meat stores and house-made traditional products like chipped beef and canned bologna that most of us had thought were consigned to the history books.

Walk past the coolers filled with (artisan, local) sodas and racks of chips and pretzels and start at the freezer. This is where all the meats that have vanished from supermarkets have come to rest. There is goose (although not from local farms), capon, and all the offal that only enthusiasts eat these days. Then check out the display case. It begins with big pieces of red meat and works its way over to the most labor-intensive artisan items: hams, puddings, and of course, scrapple (see p. 172).

When I spotted a sealed package of pig stomach, I had to know if I was looking at a portion of the Pennsylvania Dutch classic dish (imagine a giant thick slice of warm *mortadella* with gravy) or an actual washed and folded stomach of a slaughtered pig. Before I could even finish the question, a woman popped out from behind the counter and announced to everybody within earshot that she had just been to a dinner where her host made a stuffed pig stomach from scratch. She reeled off the ingredients as a kind of answer. This is the thing you buy when you make it yourself.

Dietrich's Meats is filled with the sorts of products that can be sublime at the rare butchers that make them well and a bland, greasy mess when they fail. No retail store does it better than Dietrich's. Fresh meats are cut, displayed, and packed with neat precision and their smoked products show an attention to tradition that is rare even for Pennsylvania.

Look at how the steaks are trimmed. Enough fat so they do not dry out and lean enough so you do not feel like you are buying suet. (Of course you can buy suet here.) Take a risk and taste the liverwurst and tongue souse—foods that were once commonly eaten and rejected only because their industrialized versions had the deliciousness sucked out of them. It is the same with the hot dogs. Who even thinks of shop-made hot dogs? Of course you take a risk when you buy them—it is entirely possible you will never eat one of those slick, pink commercial hot dogs again ever.

Once you have worked your way across the store, you will see jars of pickled meats. They are the ultimate time machine—pressed tripe, pig's knuckles, goose gizzards, and pieces of ring bologna. Yes, they are a bit strange looking, but for our ancestors, they were among the greatest of food luxuries. In the days when the rich had fresh and nobody had frozen, there was only salted or pickled for the rest of us. You do not have to buy them or eat them, but you do have to ponder them. I insist you take a few moments to remember how food once came into our lives.

The crew here often has a serious edge that is mistaken for rudeness by some. These are passionate craftspeople! This may be nothing more than lunch to some customers, but for the Dietrich's team—this is their whole life. Respect their product and you will respect them as people. Believe me, they will appreciate that and share their vast knowledge with you.

On the way out, take a look at the big display of smoked bones meant for dogs. For most shoppers this will be a rare moment when you will be jealous of dog food. That does not happen too often.

DOVE SONG DAIRY

BERKS COUNTY
108 SEIGFREID RD., BERNVILLE, PA 19506;
DOVESONGDAIRY.ORG; (610) 488-6060

Among Pennsylvania artisan food fans, Dove Song Dairy is famous for its goat cheeses.

You will find them all at the little farm shop—from hard, aged wedges that remind you of something from Spain or Portugal to soft, spreadable tubs that have more than a passing resemblance to cheeses you would find in France. Add a feta to the mix, check out the freezers filled with pastured meats from their animals, and it all adds up to a good reason to visit.

Dove Song Dairy is in the capable hands of Lena Schaeffer, her husband, and grown children. Indeed, her husband's ancestors built

the farm back in the eighteenth century. It hasn't always been in the family though and was re-purchased in the late forties for eight grand. That sum included forty-seven acres of land and buildings too.

When you give Lena's cheeses a taste, you are struck by how vivid they are. Not the game-y flavor you may think of if you have never tasted goat products, but a bright complexity that comes from exploring the potential of raw milk, live bacteria, and aging time.

Today, the farm greets you with the sight of great age and proper care. Every detail looks thought out, and every grazing animal appears to be content. Not polished enough to be a tourist trap, but nice enough to

The farm at Dove Song Dairy in Bernville

make you want to pull out your camera when you get there.

So where is Dove Song Dairy? It is west of Reading and just a bit north of Lancaster. The location—not far from I-78 and remote enough to require deliberate effort in order to find—is reason enough in itself to visit. It is not in Amish country and not in coal country either. There are not any mountains to be seen, and yet, it is not far from the Appalachian Trail. I was delighted. This was a pastoral farm that is quite a distance from the nearest tourist.

The heart of the dairy is its 250 goats. At any given time, about 110 of them are milking—enough for steady cheese production. Lena insists that each milker has its own name. Of course, some of you will ask for examples, so she offered Amarillo, Butterfly, Gremlin, Scamp, and Samurai. This is just the sort

Dove Song's goats

of list that leaves me scratching my head. Can you tell me which of those names is not also an automobile? Hint: It is an auto part anyway; a kind of door you will find on fancier, more exotic cars.

While all of the goats were born on the farm, it is not an entirely closed herd. An occasional male—known as a "buck"—is brought in to help with breeding and genetic diversity. This is important for animal health and happiness too. Goats do better if they grow up where they are born.

Goats, farmers, and food shoppers are all happy at Dove Song Dairy. Not far from the highway and a long drive north of Lancaster County and its tourists, it is a perfect place for a thriving small farm. Sure, there is not much around, but that is the idea.

EASTON FARMERS' MARKET

NORTHAMPTON COUNTY
CENTRE SQUARE, EASTON, PA 18042;
EASTONFARMERSMARKET.COM; (610) 330-9942

Farmers have been coming to Centre Square in Easton and selling their produce for quite a long time. In fact, they have been here steadily since 1752—this is the oldest outdoor farmers' market in America. When the first vendor set up here, Pennsylvania was a British colony and the Amish were modernists.

Come here any Saturday morning from late spring through Thanksgiving and you will find white tents set up on that same town square. Unlike most small-city farmers' markets, the farmers are the main attraction. There are no banks or utility companies and nobody hawking reusable plastic containers. Instead, you will find vendors for locally grown fruit, vegetables, and meat. A handful of artisan bakers, brewers, and distillers round out the scene.

On a nice day, you can do your weeks' food shopping, then grab a coffee and relax. There is live music, plenty of seating, and if you look straight due east down Northhampton Street, a view of New Jersey. This is as close to New York City as you can get and still be in Pennsylvania.

Easton has a market house too, it is just that it is not a crumbling building with old guys selling pretzels and pre-fried chicken, it is a brand-new space in a former downtown retail store with angular, contemporary, post-industrial décor and the sorts of products you would expect to see in Manhattan: re-invented ramen, fancy chocolates, coal oven pizza, fresh meat, fish, and espresso. There's even a teaching kitchen.

This may not be the sort of shopping you would think of doing at a seasonal outdoor farmers' market; it is a destination of its own though. In bad weather, you could pick up some meat, fish, or vegetables; have a coal oven pizza, a beer, a bowl of ramen, or a coffee drink, and wind up spending the afternoon.

I could not help but notice that the word "local" is used too often. Sitting at the ramen counter, even the bottles of sriracha sauce set out in front of me were labeled "local." This got me a bit riled up. Local tomatoes? A joy. Local eggs? A special treat. Local southeast Asian style hot sauce?

A person in a cynical mood could wander the aisles and try to count the number of times the word "local" is used here. Maybe it could be some sort of game. But there is no way to be cynical here; a pizza, a beer, or a bowl of ramen would cheer up just about anybody. How could you still have that angry edge surrounded by adults who crave noodles and children who love pizza? I left feeling happy that a thriving food scene was taking hold here.

The downside? That would be parking. Easton's gentrifying downtown has a feature no other gentrified town ever dreamed of: a theme park. Called The Crayola Experience and set in what appears to be a few re-purposed office buildings. This is probably the only farmers' market in America that combines low, rural American food prices with theme-park-high parking fees.

As it happens, the "Experience" is far more well-known than the city of Easton itself. So, any Saturday nice enough to visit the market will also be a nice enough day for carloads of families to visit too, and you compete with them head-to-head for every last space.

Do not say I did not warn you.

The scene at the Easton Farmers' Market

ELEVEN OAKS FARMS

CUMBERLAND COUNTY
23 FRYTOWN RD., NEWVILLE, PA 17241;
ELEVENOAKSFARMS.COM; (717) 805-2819

What would make a full-grown adult take up farming in the twenty-first century? And we're not talking a small plot of organic vegetables either, Eleven Oaks Farms has roughly five hundred head of cattle on almost six hundred acres—certainly not somebody's hobby. It is yet another example of farming being re-invented. The trajectory is familiar; family farm to hobby farm and back to modern farm offering a product virtually never been seen in Pennsylvania before.

It is run by its owner, Jim Schuster, his son Mallie, and Todd Lebo. I asked Todd how he describes himself and he told me, "I do not have a title. I do not know if we are big enough for me to wear one hat. We get the job done." Spoken like a guy who has spent some time farming.

What they do there is raise beef from Japanese cattle breeds. People throw the words "*waygu*" and "Kobe" around pretty often when they are talking about really expensive meat and before we do the same, we'd better review the definitions. First, there is "*waygu*," that is the Japanese word for cattle breeds that come from Japan. The meat from these animals has a distinct flavor and texture that can be enhanced with special feed and farming practices. "Kobe" is a breed of *waygu*, and a kind of beef in itself. The two are often mentioned together—or even interchangeably—but they are quite different.

Eleven Oaks raises the ones called *waygu,* not Kobe or any other sub-variety and without the codes that Asian imports get. There is no such thing as Eleven Oaks "A5." In a sense, this is not all that big a jump from the Angus animals we see everywhere, and yet, there is so little *waygu* being produced here in the states that it could be seen as revolutionary. They do it with a nod toward American consumers—their meat is destined to become steaks and roasts cooked in the American style. They do not offer the meat you see that looks like a solid block of fat with tiny pink specks of protein. Their meat shows the vivid flavor of Japanese breeds with a texture that will work on a backyard grill.

While other farmers have spent years or even decades deciding what to specialize in, Jim made up his mind over dinner one night at a restaurant in Key West. He saw *waygu* on the menu, noted the high price, and watched the way people at tables around his were ordering it up anyway. He tried one himself—it was the best steak he'd ever had. He wanted another one the following day and went back to the same restaurant, it was sold out.

Soon he was raising *waygu* cattle. No, they do not feed them beer or give them massages. They do have a diet strong on barley, a grain few American cows eat in quantity. Actually, this business of feeding a cow beer is something of a myth. Todd asked me to consider how much beer you would need to keep a herd of thousand-pound animals inebriated and I realized how impossible it was. This left me a tiny bit disappointed. I had always imagined that Japanese beef cattle staggered around their pastures dead drunk.

A raw, flatiron steak made from Eleven Oaks wagyu beef

I put their claims of taste and tenderness to the test. I bought an Eleven Oaks flatiron steak and cooked it in a cast iron skillet over high heat. Raw, it looked only a tiny bit less lean than the same cut from a supermarket meat case. Cooked, it took on an almost rust colored sear. Used to grass-fed beef, I expected a whole different eating experience, and I was right. The Eleven Oaks steak was milder, and far more tender. It was a piece of meat that was easy to love.

This is beef for steak fans. If there is nothing you crave more than a slab of beef so pure that any sauce would ruin it, this is your choice. The steaks are an experience all of you fanatics should try at least once.

ENRICO BISCOTTI

ALLEGHENY COUNTY
2022 PENN AVE., PITTSBURGH, PA 15222;
ENRICOBISCOTTI.COM; (412) 281-2602

Enrico Biscotti is one of those old school Italian businesses that seems to be a cornerstone of the Strip District. Once a neighborhood of food markets and wholesalers, the Strip now has just a few too many Steel City souvenir shops for comfort. Yes, there are biscotti—those long, crunchy cookies meant for dipping in coffee—and plenty of them. If you are new on the Strip, Enrico's looks like it has been there for a century, but it only goes back to the early nineties.

Walk into this small brick home/shop wedged in right next to two other famous Pittsburgh strip businesses. It is warm, a tiny bit dark, and surprisingly comforting. When you visit Enrico Biscotti, there is none of the intimidation that seems to infect its neighbors. The staff is really helpful, prices are reasonable, and the products are recognizable.

Well . . . most of the time anyway.

On my first visit, there was a tray of something that looked like croissants made out of pizza dough. I was baffled. They turned out to be a take on West Virginia's state food, the pepperoni roll. Invented as a portable meal for coal miners almost a hundred years ago, they are typically made with shiny, soft bread these days. Not at Enrico's! Theirs had enough crust and chewiness for a passionate bread enthusiast. I was impressed.

The pepperoni rolls piqued my curiosity but the big round loaves of bread really grabbed my attention. Indeed, they stole the show. I was supposed to be charmed by all those biscotti and I was not. Could biscotti—even banana walnut, black forest, or white chocolate macadamia flavored—hold a candle to the shelves of perfect bread in one corner of the store?

I had promised those biscotti as a gift and picked up a loaf of the bread instead. What I was buying was called "Rustic Italian Bread" and that is what it was. Unlike so much that poses as being from the boot-shaped country, it was unmistakably Italian. That dome shape was classic Europe and the crust the color of good boot leather. There was some heft when I picked it up and a bit of resistance from my bread knife when it came time to cut it. It was the real thing.

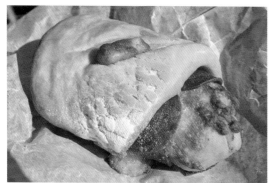

Top: The Strip District in Pittsburgh, home to Enrico's Biscotti; bottom left: A loaf of Enrico's legendary bread; bottom right: Enrico's take on the Pepperoni Roll, the state food of nearby West Virginia

This puts those biscotti in a funny position. I enjoy dunking a *biscotto* in a cup of good, strong coffee as much as the next guy. I love the way they go from hard to soft in just a moment and how all those flavors combine in a bite. Biscotti are useful. Because you can easily pack them up, they are something you can offer as a gift or take with you without worrying too much about spoilage. And those different flavors make choosing difficult, but they can also be perfect for fans of specific tastes.

And how were those biscotti? Well, I was so taken by the pepperoni rolls and rustic loaves that I forgot to try them!

THE FARMHOUSE KITCHEN

BERKS COUNTY
426 PENN AVE., WEST READING, PA 19611;
THEFARMHOUSE-KITCHEN.COM; (484) 869-5193

If somebody asked you what part of Pennsylvania had the most amount of small farms and food artisans, you would almost certainly say "Lancaster" or "Bucks County." Both are places that have long been agrarian getaways for escaping city dwellers. And yet, when you tally things up, Berks County leads the way.

The Farmhouse Kitchen is a restaurant in West Reading that celebrates local foods and their producers. Do not be fooled by the name, its setting is as city as it comes. It is on a street of boutiques, restaurants, and small shops so urban that it represents a serious parking challenge. It is exactly the sort of place you would expect to find in New Hope or Lititz, and instead, it is in Berks—a place far less celebrated.

Berks County—the area that includes and surrounds the city of Reading—is not really a getaway for anybody, and because of that, there is quite a bit of inexpensive farmland.

Between the older producers who haven't been pushed out by condo development and young newcomers taking over places left fallow a generation ago, things are coming back to life. For starters, there is Dietrich's Meats (see p. 58) to represent the old-timers, Valley Milkhouse (see p. 208), and Funny Farm Apiary (see p. 71) showing what can be done by enthusiastic newcomers.

Look at the menu and get thrown for a loop. Forget Bucks County! It seems a whole lot more like Brooklyn. Simple dishes like egg sandwiches and modern classics like avocado toast are often listed with the home farms of their main ingredients. It is pretentious at first glance, then the real vibe of Berks County kicks in. Locals think *How many of these farmers do I know?* and visitors to the area could ask, *How many of them can I visit and shop at?* It all becomes a heartfelt salute to neighboring farms.

The Farmhouse Kitchen was created by Martie Samuel, a woman who came to the restaurant business later in life. For her, it has been all about celebrating the bounty of farming. It works; the food is pure and clean in the most modern sense. Have a meal here and find out what eggs, salad, or other basics are supposed to taste like. Even though the place is on an urban street, you will come away feeling like you have stumbled onto an island of gastronomy in an ocean of farms.

No matter what, you cannot escape reality. Reading may not be the most encouraging of Pennsylvania's small cities, but this restaurant is there to tell you that the surrounding area is ground zero in the local agriculture revolution. The food served here is, more than anything, a reminder that for once the farmers are in control.

The Feast of the Seven Fishes

Standing outside in Scranton a few nights before Christmas, I was wishing for a cup of hot coffee, but instead I was on a long line in a supermarket parking lot. It is the time of year when coal country prepares for The Feast of the Seven Fishes—the Christmas Eve meal most locals see as the region's gastronomic highlight.

We were all buying fish. Indeed, fish are so important here on Christmas Eve that markets set up special kiosks out on the sidewalk or in parking lots for the occasion. Begun by Italian grocers before the days of cheap refrigeration, the outdoor stalls remain as a tangible expression of regional tradition. The big fish feast on Christmas Eve; The Feast of the Seven Fishes continues to thrive.

It is tough to know its history. In some parts of Italy, there was a seafood meal called "*la Vigilia*" before Midnight Mass, it did not include counting the dishes as part of the meal though. The number seven seemed to have made its appearance somewhere in North America and quickly became part of the event.

Today, the Feast can include dishes from just about any part of the world that sent men into the mines. You will see luxuries like lobsters and scallops; memories of crushing Appalachian poverty like smelts and sardines; old Italian favorites like octopus, eel, conch (always called by its Italian name "*scungilli*") squid; and even things that wouldn't have been known back in the day, like tilapia.

These Italian roots run deep in Scranton, and they only grow deeper in the surrounding smaller towns of Dunmore, Old Forge, and Pittston. Cooks there will be ransacking the few remaining Italian stores and making sure they have what they need.

The rest of the country may have something else on their mind, but here in the valley that runs between Scranton and Wilkes Barre, everybody is thinking fish. Buying it, cooking it, and eating it. They will gather in groups and celebrate—not just Christmas Eve—but the fact that they have made it through another year and are still sitting down at the table together.

FUNNY FARM APIARY

BERKS COUNTY
17 OAK RD., MERTZTOWN, PA 19539;
FUNNYFARMAPIARIES.COM; (610) 401-8317

My conversation with Wendy at Funny Farm Apiary began with a strong statement. She told me that bees always worked together and did their jobs without being told and went on to mention that she wished humans were that way too. I was dumbfounded. I saw bees buzzing away many times before and was (and remain) convinced that while they are indeed building hives, they are spending their days gossiping, bickering, and generally wasting time and energy. It was an existential disagreement. She wanted humans to act more like bees and I thought we were already doing a good job of it.

Maybe it is true. Bees may well be better at staying on task than humans, and they may be better at learning their jobs too. All that buzzing never seemed like orderly effort to me though. Of course, she was a highly experienced beekeeper with more than eighty hives, so it is best to take her word for it.

For most of her life, Wendy hated bees, wasps, hornets, and any other creatures in that family. Her husband, something of an amateur beekeeper, had been urging her to check out his hives and she had been refusing for years. It was approaching his birthday and she needed to get him a gift. She was newly unemployed and he was seriously overworked, so buying something was out. Instead, she mustered up her courage and offered to visit the hives as a sort of gift.

Wendy regretted this offer, but it was already out there and could not be taken back. Soon, she was the one who got a gift; it was one of those white beekeeper suits with the net helmet. This was serious. There was no way to quit now that she had the outfit.

Properly armored, she made her first trip to the hives and got a big shock—those bees were fascinating. This was the moment! She expected menacing chaos. Instead, the bees were calm, organized, and did their jobs. At that instant, she saw how hard they worked and how they communicated with each other. Wendy may have felt unemployed and a bit aimless before, but now she had a passion: beekeeping.

Her problems were not behind her yet. She still had to overcome the fact that she did not like honey. So, she grabbed some cinnamon and infused a batch of honey with it. The flavor was a bit more toler-able. And what is more, other people who wanted to add honey to their diets and did not care for the taste liked it too. Wendy was on a roll. She infused honey with blueberry, lavender, vanilla, orange, and even bourbon. Between those hard-working bees and her range of flavors, she had a product line.

Things were getting crazy down on the farm. There was a family, barnyard animals, beehives, and merchandise to sell. One day, Wen-dy's oldest son watched in awe as this new busyness engulfed him. He declared that the place was becoming a funny farm. The name was born.

These days, you can buy Funny Farm honeys, beeswax, and pol-len at several notable shops in Berks County. Check out The Nesting Box (see p. 138) and Dietrich's Meats (see p. 58) among many others. And if you are the sort of person who wants to visit the bees and see for yourself just how enterprising and conversational they are, give *Funny Farm* a call, tours are frequently available.

GREEN ZAMEEN FARM

BUCKS COUNTY
602 MINSI TRAIL, PERKASIE, PA 18944;
GREENZAMEEN.WORDPRESS.COM; (513) 348-9293

Sometimes you walk through a huge farmers' market like Headhouse in Philadelphia (see p. 84) and spot a tiny stand. You'd think that these little farms would get lost there. After all, there are vendors with whole trucks of inventory and four or five people working behind the counters. Those smaller tables make you look though. Is there something unique? Better? More special?

That is what I was asking when I stumbled upon Green Zameen Farm. I loved the way those two words came together—"green" is always a great word to have in a farm name, and "*zameen*?" It seemed Hindi to my ear and it turned out to be Urdu and Farsi too. In all those languages, it means "Earth." Even better, it is owned by a woman named Tasmeen. It is an upbeat sound that gives her work a positive feeling. Say, "Tasmeen from Green Zameen!" out loud when you meet her and you will both be smiling.

You won't see lots of variety at the Green Zameen table. Other farms could bring twenty kinds of tomatoes, hundreds of bushels of apples, or cheeses made from their own sheep, while Green Zameen offers only a few choices. There are salad greens—fresh and vibrant leaves that are never packed before you choose them, fresh herbs, and maybe a few other choices too; baby chard, bitter melon, or *gongura*. Those last two are a nod to the farm's South Asian roots.

So how did Tasmeen, the very Midwestern daughter of an engineer, wind up as a farmer in Bucks County? It is quite a story, but at least it is a love story. She was working on a farm in Ohio and wound up marrying a guy with a tree nursery here in Pennsylvania. He was happy to have a bride who wanted to farm on his property and she was pleased to discover that his location had great access to some very busy and active farmers' markets.

Tasmeen was soon selling at two. There was the Headhouse Market in downtown Philly and the Lansdale Farmers' Market in Montgomery County. Both served affluent and demanding customers and forced her to think hard about how to approach them. As she told me, "We've decided to specialize more because other people do stuff so well . . . "

She assumed her Pakistani ethnic background would attract South Asian customers, and it did, to a certain extent. For them, she offers *gongura* and bitter melon, two favorites from the region. They were not what caught on though—what customers loved were her baby lettuces, and even things she did not really know, like baby chard. It was a market table filled with green.

This was quite a learning experience. The pressure of selling among far more seasoned and successful producers gave Tasmeen a quick education. Her imagined South Asian specialty farm morphed into one producing salad greens and herbs—foods every cook needs.

Why would anybody buy baby salad greens from a farm stand when packaged equivalents are commonly available? That packaging is the issue. Small households do not need supermarket quantities and do not want the plastic waste either. Of course, these farm-grown vegetables taste better too, but you will not know that until after you have bought them.

Lots of people think you have to be a vegetable expert to shop in farmers' markets and sometimes the knowledge you overhear can be intimidating. Tasmeen told me about a time when she offered egg-plants. A child stopped, carefully checked one out, and exclaimed, "An eggplant! I did not know it was a real thing! I thought it was just an emoji!" It was a great first lesson in cooking.

GUANTE FAMILY RESTAURANT & GUANTE CAFE

JUNIATA COUNTY
2218 WILLIAM PENN HWY. (CAFE) &
111 BRIDGE ST. (RESTAURANT), MIFFLINTOWN PA 17059;
GUANTEFAMILY.COM; (717) 436-0060

If you asked me to describe a restaurant in the tiny village of Mifflintown (population 936 according to Wikipedia), I would probably guess, it would have a counter and some booths, and a menu that concentrated on eggs, burgers, coffee, and pies. That is what I imagined. No such restaurant exists in Mifflintown—at least that I could find. What they have though, is Guante Family Restaurant, a storefront with a low-key dining room and an eclectic pan Latin American menu.

This place is completely unexpected. If you are driving east from State College or north and west from Harrisburg, you will be pretty happy it is there. What you get is a comfortable room with table service and well-cooked food at reasonable prices—something not so easy to find in a remote place like this. It is the food stop you did not know you needed until you have had a meal there. The existence of Guante Family Restaurant is a pretty big surprise. Indeed, you will spend a lot of time wondering how it got there.

There are few real clues. During the course of several visits, I kept asking whoever was there how the restaurant came to be, and the best answer I could get was, "It is a long story." None of the family photos and artifacts that decorate so many Pennsylvania immigrant restaurants exist here. Indeed, there is no evidence that this is an immigrant restaurant in the first place. The menu does not give much away. There is *mofongo* with chicken, pork, or beef representing Puerto Rico; tacos and burritos carrying the Mexican banner; and sides of *curtido*, the pickled cabbage dish from El Salvador.

I had to try the *mofongo*, and pork seemed like the best of the options. After all, anybody who has driven the back roads of Puerto Rico will have seen the roadside pork stands. What came was a cast aluminum pot, its insides lined with sliced and fried plantains that formed a bowl that held a hefty helping of pulled pork in a rich, mild

A serving of the Puerto Rican favorite mofongo *with shredded pork at Guante Family Restaurant in Mifflintown*

sauce. It was a fancy presentation that seemed both welcome and wrong in this small-town storefront.

After a few bites, I did not really care. It was a great *mofongo*. I mixed the plantains, pork, and sauce together in that pot and finished it off all too quickly. I was also happy for another reason, *mofongo* is classic Puerto Rican—a mild and under-appreciated cuisine.

It was not the only beautiful plate coming out of the kitchen. Everything the server carried had some appeal. Even toddlers checked out the food. This is an eccentric culinary tour of Latin America, not a snapshot of a cuisine. You can have a grilled shrimp salad, tacos with fillings that are unknown in Mexico, or *papusas*. The menu changes, the pleasant, modest small-town setting stays the same.

Eating at Guante, I somehow mentally drifted to the Latin Caribbean. It is not that Juniata County is a bad place to be—indeed, Guante may not be near any big cities, but it is only a few minutes' drive from the Juniata Produce Auction (see p. 37). Take in both in one day for one of the most intense Pennsylvania culture shock a person can have.

A bit more than a mile west of town you will find Guante Cafe in an old, repurposed building. Here they serve coffee, tea, sandwiches, and salads. With gray cement floors, white walls, a few tables, chairs, and couches, it is the emptiest, most bare-bones coffee shop you will ever see. Do not be put off! It may not offer the food that its namesake restaurant does, but there is quality coffee and sandwiches made on good bread. It is a tiny island of flavor right off a very remote highway.

Actually, we can take it a step further. Guante Cafe is the only place for miles around where you can enjoy the amenities of a modern coffee shop. Sit down, use the restroom, check your email, and have a cup of that coffee or a sandwich. If you want more of a meal, you will almost certainly be directed to that other Guante—the restaurant in the middle of town—otherwise, come here and take a break.

THE HAINES SHOE HOUSE

YORK COUNTY
197 SHOE HOUSE RD., HELLAM, PA 17406,
HAINESSHOEHOUSE.COM, (717) 683-6328

If you are driving down Route 30, just west of Lancaster County and not quite near the city of York, there is a shoe on the south side. Three stories high and with a few windows on each floor, it is a big reminder of, well, shoes. This was not built recently. If it was, it would be a sneaker or a stiletto heel, it is not though. Today, that shape would be called a "work boot." Back in the forties, it was just a "boot."

It is The Haines Shoe House, built as a publicity stunt, preserved as a bit of history, and used today as an ice cream shop and snack bar. I get it in a way—why wouldn't a guy who made millions selling shoes build a sort of civic-minded monument to himself?

Mahlon N. Haines came to York after selling shoes with his mom in Washington, DC and set up shop. It was not quick or easy, but soon enough, he had fifty shoe stores, three kids, and a wife. He named himself "Haines, the Shoe Wizard" and pulled off every publicity stunt he could think of. Of course, that included building a giant shoe over-looking the bustling Lincoln Highway.

Not just any shoe. This one was a free resort for either honey-mooners or couples celebrating their fiftieth anniversaries. If you

The Haines Shoe House, a great place to stop for a scoop of ice cream on a summer afternoon

stayed there, you got room, meals, use of a car, and uniformed woman driver, and naturally a free pair of Haines shoes.

Your tour guide will tell you The Shoe House is five stories high, but that is really stretching it. Many three-story houses in nearby towns are taller, but the interior is split into five different levels, often with just a handful of steps between them.

In the early fifties, when The Shoe House was at its publicity-generating peak, it must have been quite a place. This sort of roadside architecture was both humorous and cutting-edge. Staying in the shoe was modern; but not for long. Radio and television became the chosen forms for advertising and suddenly, The Shoe House was a relic.

When Mrs. Haines passed away, Mahlon pretty much abandoned the shoe business and went to Paris. He re-married, gifted his stores to their long-serving managers, and lived to a healthy old age. The Shoe House did not do as well. It quickly fell into sad decay.

During the eighties, Pennsylvania became more interested in its recent history and the old buildings that once defined the experience of the Lincoln Highway were being given a second chance. The Shoe House was a perfect candidate for restoration. Solidly built and fun to see, it did stints as a snack bar and antique store. Its former guest space even became a rental apartment. Today, it is a classic spot—a Lincoln Highway icon that is still doing something useful for passing travelers.

This may not be Pennsylvania's most ambitious ice cream shop, but it is easily the most entertaining. Park your car, stand in front, and look up at the shoe. Check out the stained-glass windows with shoe images and take a selfie in front of the shoe-shaped doghouse out back. This is an eccentric bit of real Americana you just have to relish.

These days, there is nothing more than ice cream, canned soda, and bottles of water, but still, there is not another shoe in Pennsylvania that offers even that. It is much better than a convenience-store cooler. Of course, fifty years from now, those convenience stores could be museums too.

If the shoe is not enough for you, there is a big coffee pot one hundred and thirty miles west in Bedford. That building sits in the middle of a little park—a recognized piece of history, but still sadly empty. For years, I had the fantasy of putting a serious espresso bar in it, roasting coffee beans out back and warmly greeting coffee fans as they got off the turnpike for shots of my brew. The coffee pot remains unused. Let's just say it is not the only coffee dream of mine that never happened.

Foods to Look For: Hálušky

Hálušky is coal country comfort food—a mixture of egg
noodles, cabbage, onions, and butter that becomes a whole,
one-pot meal when times are tough. Then, if things get better,
it is somehow a perfect side dish for any main course. It has
roots all over Eastern Europe where both recipes and spellings
vary widely.

Do not be put off by the way the name is written. *Hálušky*
can also be rendered as *haluska, haluski, halushki,* or even
galuska. Those words describe different dishes in Europe, but
in Pennsylvania, they represent a mixture of cooked onions,
cooked cabbage, and wide noodles all brought together in a
frying pan. Bacon or kielbasa are rare options and potatoes—
which can substitute for noodles on the other side of the
Atlantic—did not seem to make the trip across the ocean at all.

It may have foreign origins, but it thrives because it is made
with ingredients that are available locally. Flour, eggs, cabbage,
and onions were easily found even in the most isolated of
mining towns. When the age of supermarkets began, these
were among the cheapest things you could buy. Flour and
cabbage can go a long way. And while bacon may have been a
luxury in the old country, it had morphed into something cheap
by the time it found its way into coal town cookpots.

Pennsylvania-style *hálušky* is not just from Eastern Europe.
Its use of noodles puts it in the same family as Italian/American,
and when you see those noodles fried with cabbage, you
cannot help but note that Chinese cooks in the area did the
very same thing.

I do not think you will need a formal recipe if you are
making *hálušky* at home. It is just that squeezing deliciousness
out of these simple ingredients takes serious time. Start with
a big frying pan, three tablespoons of butter, and four cups of
sliced onion. Put the pan over low heat—never hotter—melt
the butter and add the onions. Cook them until they are soft
and golden, this means at least an hour. Then mix in four cups
of coarsely chopped cabbage and do not turn up the heat.
Another hour later, the cabbage will be soft and the onions
intensely sweet and buttery. Season with a teaspoon of salt and

Cooking up a batch of halušky

a half teaspoon of pepper. Finally, mix in three cups of cooked, wide, egg noodles and toss them as if you were stir-frying. Do not turn up the heat though. You will burn the butter and turn the noodles to glue. Serve them right away.

Any hacks? You can modernize the dish by using savoy cabbage and gluten-free or whole-wheat noodles. Or you can make the meat version by adding chopped up pieces of bacon or kielbasa alongside the onions at the very beginning. Just remember that this is an easy dish, but not a quick one. Go slow and make sure nothing burns. Serve it, eat it, and savor it. *Halušky* returns your respect. It fed generations of Pennsylvanians and it can do the same for you.

HAY CREEK BREAD

BERKS COUNTY
ROBESON TOWNSHIP, PA;
HAYCREEKBREAD.COM

Hay Creek Bread is as much about tradition as it is about baking. Everything it does is informed by how bread was made in Pennsylvania a couple of centuries ago. Their products are all sourdough leavened and baked in a wood-fired outdoor oven. Hilary Fraley, the owner and baker, sees herself as part of a long bread making tradition with a foot in the past and the other at the present cutting edge.

Hilary has bread in her blood, or at least flour in her bones. Not only has she been around bread baking for as long as she can remember, her ancestor, Fredrick Fraley, was a baker at George Washington's Valley Forge encampment. After the war, he returned to Philadelphia and kept baking. During the yellow fever epidemic of 1793, he stayed in town, turning out loaves for as long as he could. Given that we talked at the height of the 2020 Covid pandemic, there was some serious pride and inspiration that this bit of history carried. Fredrick Fraley was about baking during good times and bad, and Hilary is the same today.

How does a person like this get their start? Much of her youth was spent in Chester County with a family cook who had a passion for baking. She learned from her, and she also learned from the time her family spent in Switzerland, followed by trips to France where she got to pick the brains of serious bakers.

It was in Europe that she came upon her philosophy of bread, as both a pure food and something for everybody to eat. There, the idea of village ovens first caught her attention. They were a place where people gathered to bake—to create this most basic of foods—and build a community. Hilary's exact words? "I wanted to bake bread for my neighbors and friends in a local and grassroots way."

Outdoor bread ovens where once the norm. Two centuries ago, they were a common sight in both Europe and North America. They would be fired up on a given day, and women would bring their dough to them. Today, they are found only among the most passionate of bakers. Hilary built her own. She started with the classic Alan Scott design and made a few modifications. Her bread is as much her recipe for brick stone and firewood as it is her recipe for flour, salt, and water.

All this makes her a member of what is sometimes described as "the bread revolution." That is . . . a movement toward breads with more taste and texture produced in small shops instead of large commercial bakeries. This change seems to be piggybacking on the farmers' market explosion. These days, you will see tables piled high with artisan breads right alongside vegetables, meats, and dairy products. Displayed there, loaves made the Hay Creek way; with only whole grains, salt, and water connect immediately with food-savvy shoppers.

As for the bread itself, there are a few varieties, including a rustic Italian, baguettes, ciabatta, and even a panettone. They all have the same roots though—a classic sourdough starter made with flour and water; whole wheat flour to start the whole wheat loaves and a white flour–based starter for the others.

The bread here bridges the gap between classic French and modern artisan. You could certainly call it "French sourdough" and "rustic Italian, too—indeed, Hay Creek has a bread called "Rustic Italian" in its lineup—but more than anything, it is contemporary American. Leavened with sourdough, baked outdoors in a handmade oven, and sold more often at farmers' markets than bakeries.

Like so many other artisan loaves, finding the bread from Hay Creek is a tough task. There is a listing of shops that sometimes carry it on her website, and the legendary Covered Bridge Farm Stand (at Valley Milkhouse see p. 208) gets a relatively large delivery when Hilary bakes. It is just that she is doing it herself with a limited ability to produce.

Yes, one person. One very dedicated lover of artisan baking. A woman and her oven producing a handmade product for her neighbors and her fans too. Reach out and her bread will reward you.

HEADHOUSE MARKET

PHILADELPHIA COUNTY
SOUTH ST. AND S. 2ND ST, PHILADELPHIA, PA 19147;
THEFOODTRUST.ORG/FARMERS-MARKETS/MARKET
/HEADHOUSE; (215) 575-0444

Most people would not think the residents of an area with a name like "Society Hill" would do much cooking. After all, it is right in downtown Philadelphia and near some great restaurants. If you have not seen it, it is a really nice neighborhood with blocks of well-shaded row houses and tasteful shops that exude modern, urban elegance. It is tough to imagine the locals buying sacks of vegetables, pulling out their pots and pans, and making dinner.

My faith in the place did not improve as open sightseeing buses and horse-drawn tourist carriages passed me, their guides pointing out the Headhouse Market while passengers stared—I guess most tourists want to see the natives go about their everyday lives. This is a perfect spot; much more than just a few farmers selling ears of corn and baskets of tomatoes, it is where Pennsylvania's best growers bring their finest produce.

I was not so different than those tourists. I first watched as the ocean of shoppers washed over the neighborhood, and then I drove three circles around the market before facing the reality of pay parking and pulling into the deck across the street. On Headhouse Square, parking was not something you did at the end of a trip, it was a continuous process—an endless chain of vehicles pulling in and out, going backward and forward, with one coming to a stop while another began its next journey.

Many decades of city living had trained me in the gentle art of dealing with large numbers of

A hand-drawn sign advertises produce for sale at the Headhouse Market in Philadelphia

people, and this would be one of those rare moments when I put those skills to the test. With my own car resting comfortably, I stuffed a notebook in my pocket, slung a camera around my neck, and waded into the crowd.

The toughest part of shopping at Headhouse is getting to the stands. At 10:30 on a summer Sunday morning, this was the busiest farmers' market I had ever seen—you had to choose your products quickly and push your way to the front. Many of the sellers have great spiels and are really looking forward to talking to you, but the press of customers precludes that.

They're all tomatoes—even the ones that look like peaches; an unusual summer specialty at the Headhouse Market in Philadelphia

Headhouse Market as we know it now was started in 2007. It is not the first on the site though. Off and on, there have been markets in this spot since 1745 and this area, known as Headhouse Square, has been home to a huge number of vendors. While this makes it the oldest operating market site, it is not Pennsylvania's oldest operating market. (That honor goes to the Easton Farmers' Market see p. 62) The present structure was built in 1804 and restored in 1994 and clearly appears to be designed for its current use. Indeed, it cries out for farmers and customers on the days it is empty.

Almost everything on offer is for home cooking and home eating. A July visit brought peaches, tomatoes, and zucchini. Peppers were starting, and cucumbers were out in more shapes and sizes than I knew existed. There was no shortage of greens and herbs either. Corn, the flagship of farmstand sales, was beginning to show up too. Even though there are tourists watching you shop, it is unquestionably a market for cooks.

These urban farmers' markets have a reputation for high prices, and as usual, it was not true. Sellers offered fruit, vegetables, cheese, meat, and fish of clearly remarkable quality at prices lower than what

During the summer, Headhouse Market spills out of its shelter and onto the streets of Philadelphia.

is being charged at suburban, chain supermarkets. Of course, whatever you save on ingredients, you will lose on pay parking, but it evens out in the end.

Pay special attention to dairy. Quality cheese and yogurt are expensive to produce, so this direct, farmer-to-customer model makes these urban markets the best places to buy cheese and butter. I noticed several cheese makers from my area that only sell here. In the country, nobody will pay a decent price for cheese, in the city, that same price is a bargain.

As closing time approached and the customers thinned out, I realized that everybody who sold at Headhouse was grateful for the chance. You get to live in Pennsylvania farm country all week and come to this nicest of urban neighborhoods on Sunday morning. City people may no longer welcome farmers as living food heroes the way they did a decade ago, but they are still happy enough for the chance to buy all this top-notch stuff.

It is a good deal for everybody.

HIGHLAND CHOCOLATES

TIOGA COUNTY
11724 ROUTE 6, WELLSBORO, PA 16901;
HIGHLANDCHOCOLATES.ORG; (570) 724-9334

With a name like Highland Chocolates, you would expect something with at least a touch of Scotland, there was nothing of the sort though. Just a modest store with a very powerful mission to provide meaningful work for adults with developmental disabilities. It is a calm pleasant shop staffed by people who are in a good mood.

You will find Highland Chocolates a bit east of the town of Wellsboro, deep in the mountains and not far from the Grand Canyon of Pennsylvania. There is a retail store in front and a workshop in the back. Even when there is nobody behind the counter, the shop will be buzzing; a whole crew melting, molding, mixing, and spreading chocolate. If you ask, they will show you around—it is the least intimidating food production tour in the state—the team was making Easter bunnies and nut bark while I was there.

On the tour, I was given hair and beard nets and told I would see their shaker table. No, it was not a fine New England antique; it was a metal table that shakes the bubbles out of molded caramel and chocolate pieces. Most everything else is done by hand though, barks are mixed and spread by hand, and molds are filled the same way.

Begun in 1994, Highland has been around long enough to prove its quality. Using chocolate from Van Leer, Callebaut, and Merckens, they mold, shape, and coat a wide variety of products. Many of them are seasonal. On the March day I visited, there were those Easter bunnies of course, and also shamrocks and leprechauns. They were not the only shapes, birthday-card flat slabs, gaslights that recalled Wellsboro's main street, and what I thought of as chocolate tiles were among my favorites.

Do not expect the elaborate. Tree Stumps are the most complicated item. They've got layers of peanut butter, caramel, and pretzels coated in chocolate. And then there were those favorites of mine; chocolate covered marshmallows. Bigger than most, they were so crudely coated that they reminded me of dark brown miniature cheeses—no question they were handmade and miles above anything from a factory.

What will impress visitors the most is the way chocolate here can be delicious in any form. Dip a pretzel in it, eat a few crumbs of bark, or enjoy the most elaborate of creations. The good people at Highland Chocolates do most of this for a reasonable price and offer a smile to each visitor too.

Highland Chocolates is more than a shop; it is something of an ecosystem. They make good quality sweets, they employ a friendly group of disabled adults, and, because of that, they contribute to the community in more ways than you may think. Take a tour, have a marshmallow, and enjoy.

HISTORIC ROUND BARN AND FARM MARKET

ADAMS COUNTY
298 CASHTOWN RD., BIGLERVILLE, PA 17307;
ROUNDBARN.FARM; (717) 334-1984

OYLER'S ORGANIC FARMS & MARKET

ADAMS COUNTY
400 PLEASANT VALLEY RD., BIGLERVILLE, PA 17307;
OYLERSORGANICFARMS.COM; (717) 677-8411

Turning onto a narrow farm road a few moments west of Gettysburg, you will see the Historic Round Barn. If you are one of those people who thought that round barns were confined to New England Shaker villages, you are in for a surprise. Round barns have been built almost everywhere in the US, including central Pennsylvania.

Noah Sheely and his family needed a barn and loved the whole idea of a round one. Was Noah a Shaker? There was no Shaker village anywhere near Gettysburg when this round barn was built in 1914. The woman behind the cash register told me that Noah was "of

the Shaker faith." I was not sure. I doubted a person could practice it without the communal dimension.

Instead, he seemed like the many thousands of other people who loved Shaker stuff. Only, instead of a chair or a table, he sought out  an entire barn. He went ahead, hired an architect, and built it. The result is what you see on Cashtown Road; the most beautiful farm market in Pennsylvania— maybe the most beautiful farm market in America. I spent forty minutes photographing the outside before I even went in.

It is not a museum, is not a relic of a lost Shaker village, and is not a building preserved by a non-profit. It is a real working farm with orchards and cornfields within fifty yards of the parking lot. Only instead of an old shed or those white tents, you have a round, white barn.

This is part of Pennsylvania's fruit-growing heart. Here you can buy great apples, peaches, and other seasonal farm produce. In July, I saw a good selection of green vegetables too. That is not all they sell though. There are more jars and packages than I would hope for and a large space devoted to souvenirs and gifts. It left me confused. On one hand, you would hope that a setting as stunning as this would offer more than tee shirts and baskets, and on the other, if you have to shop for local stuff, why not do it in the nicest place possible?

The Historic Round Barn is so beautiful that you really want to stick around for a while. Luckily, there is a restaurant and brewery right across the street that continues this sense of the pastoral. Indeed, those plants that look like giant grape vines are hops for their beers.

A setting like this one makes the Historic Round Barn a perfect place for weddings and other events. During the beautiful summer morning light I encountered on one visit, I could easily imagine a crew from *Vogue* setting up a photo shoot. Nothing would fit into the scene like beautiful models with perfect makeup and flowing dresses. All this elegance gave the place one more unforeseen advantage—restrooms worthy of a fine restaurant. After the traffic of Gettysburg, these were welcome.

Oyler's Organic Farms & Market is just a few miles from the Round Barn and is a quality destination in itself. The shop's freezers are filled with beef, poultry, and baked goods; coolers hold local raw milk, butter, and cheese; and shelves display vegetables and fruit. Only a small part of the shop is devoted to non-perishables and these included textbooks on artisan cheesemaking and packages of locally made pasta.

The Oyler family may not have been visionaries in barn architecture, but they have been on the land for six generations and are still going strong. Besides top-notch ingredients, there are farm dinners and cooking classes too. I could not help but think that if I wanted to cook a meal worthy of the Historic Round Barn, I would have to buy my ingredients at Oyler's.

HOMETOWN
FARMERS MARKET

SCHUYLKILL COUNTY
125 MAHANOY AVE., TAMAQUA, PA 18252;
HOMETOWNFARMMKT.COM; (570) 668-2630

The Hometown Farmers Market is not named after some romantic notion of a mythical American hometown. Actually, Hometown is the real name of the village where it is located. Do not be fooled by its proximity to Jim Thorpe or Mount Pocono, this is coal country. Everything you see here is here because of coal. The railroads, homes, businesses, and of course, the mines themselves, are its reason for existence.

Here in Hometown, you will find a few houses, a diner, and, just a tiny bit west of the crossroads that marks its center, a flea market/farmers' market that people from miles around visit. It is only open on Wednesdays, so if that is when you happen to be in the area, stop by and look around. For the locals, this is a good place to shop. It is cheaper than the big box stores and closer than the malls—a chance to buy food, clothing, tools, and housewares at low prices while visiting with neighbors and just plain getting out of the house.

Scattered among vendors selling cheap sunglasses, work gloves, and diabetic socks are traces of an Eastern European food heritage. Not just meat—everybody expects sausages for some reason—but baked goods and cooked dishes too. Grab a stack of potato pancakes and a bowl of *halušky* (see p. 80). Nobody is speaking Polish, but these foods are clues to the past. We constantly hear about Italians in the mines, but not Eastern Europeans. They were there too though. Food tells stories and cannot keep secrets.

At the Hometown Farmers Market, the smell of frying potato pancakes acts as a sort of olfactory soundtrack as you walk the grounds. Indeed, one stand selling those pancakes offered a "Polish Picnic" of them along with pierogies and *halušky*. It was not even that late in the day, but the pierogies and *halušky* were sold out already.

I drowned my disappointment with a stack of potato pancakes. They were soaked in cooking grease and way too hot to touch. I started working on them as they cooled. I skipped the toppings—they offered ketchup or grape jelly—neither seemed right in my mind. For a split second, I feared becoming one of those old guys who carries

The Hometown Farmers Market in—where else? Hometown

hot sauce with him wherever he goes. Certainly, a few splashes would have made the moment.

Walking around with my plate of potato pancakes, I saw that old CDs, vinyl albums, and tee shirts seemed to be popular items. The music you will see offered here is what people once called "album-oriented rock," a bit more serious than Top 40 but not as intellectual as jazz. Even though I am not all that much of a fan, for a second I wanted a *Yes* tee shirt. It would announce to the farmers' market world that I, too, was part of that generation and owned a few albums of my own.

I did not need a tee shirt to show I was a child of the seventies though. I stood there with all the others. My cargo pants, baseball cap, and thinning head of gray hair all helped me be one of the crowd; too old to change, too young to retire, and looking for something good to eat. It may be a bit off the beaten track, but at the Hometown Farmers Market, fitting in is easy.

INDIAN HUT EXTON AND MALVERN

CHESTER COUNTY
INDIAN HUT EXTON, 260 N. POTTSTOWN PIKE, EXTON, PA 19341;
INDIANHUT.COM; (610) 363 9500

HIMALAYAN INDIAN GROCERY & FOOD

29 MARCHWOOD RD., EXTON, PA 19341;
HIMALAYANPA.COM; (610) 524-3100

EXTONINDIAN MALVERN

490 LANCASTER AVE., MALVERN, PA 19355;
BOMBAYDHABBA.COM; (484) 855-8484

A century ago, immigrants and their neighborhoods were always urban. New arrivals crowded into big-city enclaves and did not leave until they "made it." At that point they left and never looked back. Nowadays, those urban areas are not only too expensive, but they are also not where the jobs are located. Exton and Malvern are the perfect modern immigrant towns. Their miles of suburban housing are not exactly cheap, but they are near huge office park employers and are still relatively affordable.

The result is an entirely different sort of melting pot. Distinctly Indian sorts of stores and restaurants co-mingle with the usual shopping mall brands in a mix that is intensely American in a way you may have never thought possible. Indian Hut is one of those restaurants. It is in a strip mall pretty much opposite a Whole Foods Market, and it shares the mall building with other small eateries offering falafel and Sichuan—each one reaching out to customers who are very far from home.

Indian Hut does not fool around, no matter what you order, you will get something an Indian customer would recognize as authentic. I had a *masala dosa*—the giant crepe filled with spicy mashed potatoes that is an icon of south Indian cuisine. Soon it came, a long rolled and stuffed pancake with two chutheys and a bowl of the pungent lentil and tamarind soup called *sambar* on the side. I ripped a bit of *dosa*

My dosa *and* sambar *at Indian Hut in Exton*

from one end and felt the crunch. Then I dipped it in the soup and chewed it down. It was not as complex as it could have been, but a happy *dosa* nonetheless.

A mile or so up the road, I found another strip mall with its own global twist. Clearly, this was once a typical neighborhood shopping center with a supermarket and a row of smaller stores. Today, they include Himalayan Indian Grocery & Food, with shelves of grains, a produce section, spices, condiments, and a vast array of frozen, canned, and bagged ready-to-eat Indian dishes.

Most people I know are a tiny bit intimidated by the sight of Indian grocery stores—what are those heavy bags of powders? How do you use those spices and why do you need them in such vast quantities? And what do you do with jackfruit, curry leaves, and drumsticks?

It is not just that though. Between the freezers in the back, the steam table by the register, and the shelves of jars in the middle, there are enough prepared foods and instant mixes to satisfy even the most kitchen-challenged person. Try a *kati* roll, a package of *palak paneer*, or a jar of curry paste. Microwave the frozen or follow a few simple cooking instructions on the paste jars and the flavors of India will be yours.

Like lots of people, I have a favorite food. Mine is an Indian dish called "chicken 65." and when I saw it on the menu at Bombay Dhabba in Malvern, I knew I had to get it. These bits of highly seasoned, fried boneless chicken hold potential; properly cooked, the chicken will do its usual great job of carrying strong flavors and you will be a happy diner.

With a meal of Hakka noodles, *bhindi masala*, garlic naan, and the aforementioned chicken 65 in a distinct Bombay Dhabba logo shopping bag, I sat down at a local park picnic table and spread out my haul. The fragrance was sublime, but what exactly was I eating? Hakka noodles are a favorite in Chinese restaurants in India and not really from Hakka at all, *bhindi masala* are a kind of curried okra, garlic naan is a wheat flatbread with actual whole cloves of garlic baked in, and of course, my chicken 65.

I was sitting at a picnic table of Indian culinary longing—Chinese as it is served in India, a couple of street vendor dishes, and a curry. Even though I have never been to India, I was suddenly feeling homesick for it. A few plastic containers of food were playing with my emotions and carrying me away.

Indian food holds back nothing. Spicy intensity was lurking everywhere, and each bite somehow had a whole rainbow of flavors. I was shoveling it all down while an Indian family at a neighboring picnic table watched me carefully. An old man with a huge meal and a tripod-mounted camera was not something they saw every day. I watched back. Their lunch was from a global fast-food chain and lacked the constellation of tastes available in spades at almost any Exton or Malvern strip mall.

In this area, immigrant cooking is thick on the ground, Mexican, Middle Eastern, and most of all, Indian. None of this is for tourists, and the warmest greetings are reserved for those people who know their dosas. Is that not always the story? Love the food and the people who made it will love you back.

THE JIGGER SHOP

LEBANON COUNTY
202 GETTYSBURG AVE., MOUNT GRETNA, PA 17064;
JIGGERSHOP.COM; (717) 964-9686

The Jigger Shop is an ice cream parlor in Mount Gretna, roughly half-way between Lancaster and Lebanon. Go, grab a snack, sit down, and try to get a sense of the place. Is this a resort? A town? Some combination of the two? Mount Gretna describes itself as "The Pennsylvania Chautauqua." That is a help for those of you who know your American cultural history, but not really for the rest of us.

Okay, a Chautauqua was a place people went to both relax and learn. Sort of a resort and college combined. They flourished before the days of online university lectures and specialized cruises. People came to Mount Gretna to escape the city, get some fresh air, and pick up something new. While they were there, they'd gather to talk about what they have been learning over an ice cream at The Jigger Shop."

Chautauquas may be history for most people, but they are still happening at Mount Gretna. You can come, attend a lecture, participate in a book discussion, and head over to The Jigger Shop afterward. Sure, things have changed a bit here. There is pizza, a sit-down restaurant, and even a bar with trivia nights, but the biggest crowds line up at The Jigger.

And line up they do. At two on a Monday afternoon, the wait for ice cream was almost an hour. Kids, seniors, teens, and working adults were all there and ready to order. A menu at the entrance listed

Top: A simple sign welcomes you to The Jigger Shop in Mount Gretna
Bottom: An ice cream soda from The Jigger Shop, straight out of an earlier century and right there for you

specialty sundaes and drinks. You could choose all sorts of combinations with plenty of time to make up your mind. Did I want a "Pineapple Upside Down" or "Bananas Foster" sundae?

I waited patiently. Reactions to the long line were mixed. Those of us there by ourselves normally may have passed the time studying our phones, but Mount Gretna offered little in the way of a signal. Groups that were silent the first few minutes gradually became more talkative. The family behind me eventually became so bored that they started chatting with me.

This gave me a real chance to look around. It appeared that hardly anybody was eating anything from that fancy menu. Instead, most were having simple scoops of ice cream and dishes from the separate cooked foods counter. I ordered a "Broadway," a coffee soda with chocolate ice cream and carried it to an outdoor table. With my drink in front of me, it all made sense. There were glasses, steel dishes for the ice cream, and baskets for the cooked food.

Even better, it was all for real. Actual coffee in my coffee soda, real whipped cream, and a reasonably real-seeming cherry on top. I bit in and for the first time in decades, I enjoyed an ice cream soda. I chewed on the cherry, savored the whipped cream, licked the ice cream, and sipped the soda.

Everybody around me was doing the same thing. We sat on the porch and returned to a time when there was no greater pleasure than going out to the country and having a special treat. The tables had bright red tablecloths, the view was the green landscape of Mount Gretna, and it was available to anybody who was willing to wait in line for a bit.

It was not all old. There were espresso drinks, wrap sandwiches, and customers paying with credit cards. Nonetheless, it was a Chautauqua—a scene out of time—a place to be both entertained and educated. Here was a "Hall of Philosophy" with lectures from leading scholars and a round theater that occasionally offered chamber concerts, all linked by forest paths. And all those paths led to The Jigger Shop.

JOHN'S ROAST PORK

PHILADELPHIA COUNTY
14 E. SNYDER AVE., PHILADELPHIA, PA 19148;
JOHNSROASTPORK.COM; (215) 463-1951

Philadelphia is filled with all sorts of exciting neighborhoods, each with an explosion of food cultures and interesting dishes to explore. It is just that Snyder Avenue and its patch of shopping south of downtown is not among them. All is not lost though. Head over and you will find John's Roast Pork—a little, old-school fast-food shack wedged into a patch of land surrounded by modern, chain strip malls.

It is there. As it is, and as it was. You can see that it began as a tiny kitchen. The semi-enclosed dining area that could easily be described as either indoor or outdoor was probably added later. It is the sort of honest sandwich shop that most Americans ate in before fast-food chains elbowed them aside.

A pork and spinach sandwich at John's Roast Pork

Strangely enough, the roast pork that John's is famous for is not even at the top of the menu. The top is where you will find cheesesteaks (see p. 102). They have an awkward relationship with roast pork sandwiches at best. Both began as filling workingman's meals in industrial Philadelphia. Then cheesesteaks found fame and fortune while roast pork was left back home, toiling at the same old task it had taken up decades before.

On the very long line at John's, I had plenty of time to ponder the laminated tear sheets from the *New York Times, Bon Appétit, Gourmet, USA Today*, and the *Washington Post* that graced the wall behind me. The place and its specialty were celebrated. They won a James Beard Award too. And on top of that, the local press could fill an encyclopedia. Then there was *Zagat*, and finally, there was the sandwich.

This was the home of the roast pork sandwich, but more people were going for the steaks. This place is so far off the beaten tourist path that you know they cannot offer anything unless it is popular

Foods to Look For: Cheesesteaks

There are times when a person from southeastern Pennsylvania may ask for a steak and mean a big piece of broiled or grilled meat from a cow. Not usually though. In that part of the state, "steak" more commonly means a long, sub-shaped sandwich of cooked, shredded beef, with toppings of cooked onions and melted cheese.

Even though fans talk about cheesesteaks as if the recipe is rigid, there are many variations you should know about before you order one. Options are those onions of course, hot or sweet peppers, and cheese. You do not have to have any of it, or you can have everything. The choice is yours. Of course, arguments break out. I really prefer provolone cheese to the commercial orange stuff, and I love the little cup of hot peppers that many shops keep on the side. I have gotten a few nasty looks when I ask for this, but I will tolerate them in order to get what I want, when I want it. I believe that cheesesteak shops are great places to assert your stubbornness.

In a way, this is fast food. After all, they usually can get these sandwiches out to you pretty quickly. Even so, the time it takes to go from those raw beef slices to a fully ready sandwich does not fly by. First those slices go on a flattop grill until they are brown, then the cook uses a spatula or two to break them down into shreds. At that point, they are heaped on a warm corner of the grill until they are needed. When it is time to assemble the sandwich, your cook will squirt some oil onto the flattop and re-fry the meat along with whatever you've ordered. This is when the onions, peppers, and cheese make their appearance. Hot peppers are usually on the side.

No matter what choices you make, these sandwiches are icons of local food tradition. Ordering and eating them puts your Philadelphia street cred on display. Get one and finish it off and you are on the right track. Make a mistake the way John Kerry did in 2003—when he asked for his with Swiss cheese—and your gaffe will be remembered forever.

There are extreme options that are permissible. Choose pork and broccoli rabe instead of beef (as I often do) and a small but influential minority of Philly food fans will be impressed. More contemporary steak restaurants will offer even more choices; chicken as the meat, or even no meat with a helping of grilled mushrooms taking its place.

Cheesesteaks and their fans raise a moral question in my mind— is there really a need to impress them when you are choosing a sandwich? You may

A Philadelphia style steak sandwich with tomato sauce—a personal pleasure

want to have one the perfectly "correct" way in order to get a sense of what the gurus are talking about. You may. It may make more sense to wade right into the fray and just get what you want. Ultimately, this is about you enjoying your food, not impressing the person who hands you your order.

Although they are often filled, John's outdoor picnic tables were empty the bitterly cold day I took this picture

with the locals. Look for scrapple and egg sandwiches at breakfast, and steaks and pork at lunch.

I sat down and started unwrapping my sandwich. There did not seem to be a plated, eat-in option. All the sandwiches were just wrapped in foil and sealed with masking tape, so I peeled the layers back one by one and between the sunshine pouring through a window and the reflections from wrapping, my sandwich looked like a movie star. Its beauty was crying out. The pork, the spinach on top, and the bread that supported it all were holding me in a sort of porcine rapture.

Should I take a picture? Take a bite? I did and the aroma of properly made gravy challenged the sight of the sandwich for my attention. The power was so great that my bad Philly meat sandwich memories vanished and were replaced by this intense bit of pork and its bright green spinach cap. No wonder people keep eating these sandwiches! I understood, they were trying to re-experience the moment when they had one this good.

Seating was not exactly spacious; I could see I was alone in more ways than one. I was sitting by myself with only a camera and notepad for company and I was clearly the only one eating the specialty of the house. I was crying inside.

Have the roast pork. Show the world that this great treasure of regional cuisine is something more than a sideshow. Tell me honestly if that pork does not speak to you.

JOSIE'S GERMAN CAFE & MARKET

CUMBERLAND COUNTY
5238 E. TRINDLE RD., MECHANICSBURG, PA 17055;
GERMANFOODATJOSIES.COM; (717) 697-6462

Pennsylvania Dutch Country was once a really big place. And when it was, German shops and restaurants were thick on the ground in a swath that ran from Allentown west past Harrisburg. Today, there is almost nothing left. Many locations that once served German food are now pizzerias or gone completely. This is too bad; any cuisine that represents a culture that has thrived for hundreds of years deserves our respect.

Josie's German Cakes & Market is not exactly a holdout—it has only been open since 1985. And yet, it is one of the few places that cooks and sells real German food. Walk in, check out the shelf of German-language books, and study the map of Germany for a few moments. You will not find a deep selection here, but the basics are waiting. Sauces, condiments, and pickles are on the shelves and sausages and cold cuts are in a cooler behind the dining room.

All that was missing was a German soundtrack, but that just got me wondering, would that be Wagner? Milli Vanilli? I hesitated for a moment; I am a big classical music fan and still wouldn't want to sit down to a meal with Beethoven in the background.

The big draw at Josie's is the dining room. Think of it as a sort of sausage specialty restaurant. A place where a bratwurst becomes a meal. You can have a platter with a bratwurst, a *weisswurst*, or even *wursts* with curry sauce. And do not forget liverwurst sandwiches. It is a menu of German basics that will thrill sausage fans of any level.

There are also side dishes. The potato salad has a vinegar zing and the sauerkraut a rich unctuousness, exactly the reverse of what you would expect. You can also find those German noodles called *spätzle* and red cabbage too. Is it a bit stereotyped? Yes of course, but it is also simple and straightforward. The most intimidating thing on the menu is that liverwurst. Every other sausage can be politely described as really good-tasting and similar to a big hot dog.

Come on in and take a seat. The bright yellow walls, folding chairs, and laminate tables are a reminder of the restaurants that once graced every small town in Pennsylvania. There is a local feel,

103

The bratwurst platter at Josie's

but if you check the license plates in the parking lot, you will see that many cars have come a very long way to get here.

I saw a dessert menu with plum cake and apple strudel. I skipped them though; my platter of bratwurst, potato salad, and sauerkraut with a side of spätzle was enough. That being said, Josie's also does a fair amount of serious German baking too. You can order an apple cake, black forest cake, chocolate mousse torte, German fruit torte, *kaese sahne* cheesecake, peach torte, or pineapple torte.

Josie's is one of the last survivors—a modest shop and restaurant serving German specialties. If you need a fix, you have to come, and you have to do your best to keep it alive. There are not many alternatives.

LA COLOMBE COFFEE ROASTERS

PHILADELPHIA COUNTY
1335 FRANKFORD AVE., PHILADELPHIA, PA 19125; LACOLOMBE.COM; (267) 479-1600

I confess, I am the sort of person who watches those corny cable shows. You know what I am talking about . . . the ones where the most unlikely of heroes accomplish something you are supposed to find amazing. I am also an obsessive coffee drinker and for a few seasons, there was a program that targeted me perfectly. It was called *Dangerous Grounds* and its host, a tough-talking guy called Todd Carmichael, would risk life and limb in an effort to get the very best beans for his coffee shop, La Colombe, in Philadelphia.

Never mind that other high-end coffee roasters tasked the same mission to ladies-of-a-certain-age traveling alone. Todd made the job of coffee buyer into something that 007 fans could enjoy. Nights in dank hovels, at least one daring escape by helicopter, and the constant attention of thieves and hustlers gave the show a tension that almost made me feel guilty for drinking coffee in the first place.

The red brick building that houses the headquarters of the La Colombe empire

Todd was there, always looking like he'd just spent six months on the Appalachian Trail. Only when he opened his backpack, there was a tiny portable coffee roaster and hand grinder instead of a space-age mini tent and sleeping bag. It was easy to imagine him getting that gear from some secret spy laboratory.

I was a *Dangerous Grounds* superfan. My head was exploding with all the great coffees Todd bought on the show, and as I approached the La Colombe flagship shop in the Fishtown section of Philly, I was hoping for beans from India, South America, and Africa too. I wanted more than perfect coffee; I wanted an adventure of my own.

Outside, it was on a block that was once industrial and now was all about shopping. Not groceries, socks, and underwear, but the sorts of things that cost a fortune and do not really have any use. Mostly, the stuff you would put in your house if you wanted everybody who visited to know you dropped some big bucks in a cool neighborhood. La Colombe was in the middle of it, and the signs outside read "Atelier, Cafe, Boulangerie, Distillerie." That is a lot of hip French stuff in one place.

With a tough guy like Todd in charge, I expected it to give off a barroom brawl vibe. Instead, it was extreme chic. Exposed

Coffee and a muffin at La Colombe in Fishtown

brick and wood beams, seats with mid-century modern laminate, and painted metal frames all worked together to give you the feeling that you should have dressed better. I calmed down a bit; nobody would throw a punch here.

Did you think this place was an espresso bar? It is. It is also a bakery though, with bread, muffins, and fancier pastries. Walk past the bakery and coffee bar and there is a real bar . . . one with beer and cocktails, and finally, when you are really deep in the building, there is a wood-burning pizza oven.

At a table, I was surrounded by meetings, conversations, and meals. I ordered brewed coffee in a mug, got a muffin to go alongside it, and sat down. I wanted to check some facts and quickly learned there was no Wi-Fi. Maybe this inability to work was why so many people seemed so friendly.

Everything there was exemplary. The coffee? World class. The pastries? The best I have had in a place that also served specialty coffee. Their goodness exploded the myth that great pastries and fine specialty coffee could not be served in the same place. I did not even get to the savory food. People all around me were eating salads and cooked breakfasts, and I could barely down my muffin.

Behind the public area, there were several rooms with classes and workshops. I wondered what they were studying. There was so much going on and no way to listen in. Were they learning coffee? Baking? Distilling? This is the capitol of an empire. La Colombe now has at least thirty locations and all had to be stocked with coffee of this very high quality. Maybe you really did need to go on missions to supply it.

On my way out, I noticed a corner with coffee brewing gear, hats, tee shirts, and mugs. As much as I loved the place, there was only one thing I wanted and it was not for sale—one of those tiny portable coffee roasters that Todd used on his show. It did not look like he was going to share that with anybody.

Foods To Look For: Pretzels

JULIUS STURGIS PRETZEL BAKERY, 219 E MAIN ST., LITITZ, PA 17543; JULIUSSTURGIS.COM, (717) 626-4354

Here in the Keystone State, pretzels are serious food. The rest of the world may know them as a snack that flight attendants hand you, but here, they are seen as local and traditional. Indeed, hard pretzels were invented in Lititz, Lancaster County (more about that later).

In Pennsylvania, pretzels come two ways. Hard is the bagged snack food. They can be heart-shaped, in thumbnail-sized nuggets, or in sticks of varying thickness. The biggest sticks are called "rods" and were a favorite during my New York City childhood. In their favor, hard pretzels can stay fresh for long periods without refrigeration or even preservatives.

These hard pretzels are not the only game in town. You can also find soft pretzels. They are not soft like commercial white bread, but instead, they have an outside crust like a good bagel and an inside like Italian bread. Calling both the crunchy bagged things and the soft street food "pretzels," made me think that it could be possible to define them by shape. Dough does not become a pretzel when it is twisted into hearts though.

The giant pretzel that greets you at the Julius Sturgis Pretzel Bakery in Lititz

Soft pretzels can be great if you find them freshly baked, that is a pretty big if though. All too often, they are still chewable, but on the edge of stale. Some people claim to be able to tell soft pretzel freshness by looking, but none have convinced me. I usually just avoid them—even though I wouldn't mind one on occasion.

Most pretzel recipes today have a combination of yeast and baking soda to give them that distinct texture, but this cannot be all that historic. Neither commercial yeast nor baking soda have been around that long. Before, the dough was probably leavened with sourdough and crisped in a lye bath. That is not very consistent, and lye is not the safest thing to have around a kitchen, but that is what they had.

The Julius Sturgis Pretzel Bakery in Lititz claims to be the birthplace of hard pretzels. There at their old bakery—now restored as a museum—you can see beautiful brick ovens that were once fired with wood, coal, or coke and learn about how a commercial bakery ran in the nineteenth century. Their website shows dough being hand-formed into that classic pretzel shape, but that is at the museum, not the production line.

I took the tour and was thinking hard about what sourdough-leavened and wood-fired pretzels may taste like while I was being told about modern machinery and automation. Nothing stops me from asking food questions though and I stepped right up and asked if there was any company that still hand-formed their pretzels. (Wood-firing seemed too big a stretch—even by my standards.) The tour guide, whispered, "Hammond, in downtown Lancaster."

Sturgis did not disappoint though. The handmade soft pretzels they sold by the cash register turned out to be excellent. They had real pretzel texture and bread flavor and were completely fresh. I walked away happy, but still wondering about hard pretzels.

A quick check of the Hammond website (hammondpretzels .com) showed that there was no factory tour, but a whole different process. At Hammond, cooking began with a bath in a baking soda solution—something similar to the pre-boiling that bagels go through. These pretzels were linked in one way or another to both breadsticks and bagels.

I bought a bag of each brand and took them home for further study. Let's be clear here. I was comparing grocery store examples of both. Sturgis made theirs—labeled "Dutch Style"—in a modern factory near Reading. Hammond's—just called "pretzels"—came from their bakery/shop in Lancaster. Both were heart-shaped and about the same size.

It did not take long to notice that the Sturgis pretzels were more consistent. Every one in the bag was the same exact shape and form and there were no creases where the folds of dough

Welcome to the Julius Sturgis Pretzel Bakery

intersected. At the Sturgis museum, we were told they currently use a die extrusion process to shape the dough and you could

Hard pretzels from Hammond in Lancaster

Soft pretzels from Julius Sturgis in Lititz

easily tell. The Hammond pretzels bore far more handwork. The shapes were slightly irregular, and it was hard to find more than three or four in a bag that were both identical and flawless. Like rounds of artisan cheese, there were tiny differences that you noticed.

I planned to have a small taste of both, but got carried away. Instead of tasting, I ate half a bag of each. The Sturgis pretzels were mild and the Hammond stronger. The Hammond package said nothing about sourdough and listed yeast as an ingredient, but somehow, it had a deeper flavor. There could have been a million reasons for this, but it all added up to somebody deciding that Hammond would appeal to a smaller but more passionate group of fans.

Was I among them? For a moment. And then I realized I had not even scratched the surface. Who even knew how many small-batch hard pretzel bakers there were? I shuddered to think about it.

LANCASTER CENTRAL MARKET

LANCASTER COUNTY
23 N. MARKET ST., LANCASTER, PA 17608;
CENTRALMARKETLANCASTER.COM; (717) 735-6890

It is almost the end of October and Lancaster Central Market is on the cusp. There are vendors with beautiful heirloom tomatoes—those classic icons of summer seasonality sitting right next to properly formed crowns of broccoli—a vegetable that signals autumn as surely as a reddening maple leaf.

In the minds of farmers, there is a bit of glamour in produce. The big piles and bright colors put on something of a show. That in itself is good reason to look carefully at the other vendors. Cases of dairy or poultry may not seem as exciting, but they offer high quality and good deals.

As I strolled the market, I could not help but wonder if cakes and candies were the real glam items. No carrot looked as good as a pie and even a slice of baked oatmeal could hold its own against a basket of bell peppers. Are bakeries really seasonal? Does the appearance of a pumpkin pie signify the passage of time the same way a huge stalk of Brussels sprouts does?

This change does not happen suddenly and in heavily agricultural Lancaster County, the clues are everywhere. The farmers here are good at extending the seasons—it is not like you will see peaches and eggplants one day and pears and cabbage the next. Crops overlap. With a bit of craft, there can be tomatoes that ripen in mid-October and kale that appears while it is still beach weather.

Not everything you see for sale at Lancaster Central Market is local—you must ask. Some stands represent one farm, and others may be wholesalers too. Walk the market aisle by aisle and study the day's offerings carefully. The last peppers and first Brussels sprouts may both be on display together.

All this was on my mind as I noticed the way turkeys were sneaking into the butcher counter. The poultry stand always has boneless turkey breast and something they call "turkey London Broil," a meat that is both incomprehensible and tasty at the same time. And then, you start seeing whole turkeys. Some big, some bigger, but none as wide across the front as the ones you see in the supermarket.

I tried to ask a few more serious-sounding seasonality questions when an Amish farmer/vendor started poking fun at me. "It is not that the vegetables stop growing in the cold weather, it is that our fingers get frostbitten before we can pick enough of them." He told me this while trying and failing to keep a straight face. It was a perfect example of Pennsylvania Dutch humor.

During the summer, a few new farmers had found their way into the market. This was a positive development. I was among many who feared that Lancaster Central Market was on its way to becoming a food court. There was good reason for concern; at least a few stands once held by local farmers were now selling super fruit bowls, fancy juices, or Amish souvenirs.

Actually, the place is described as a "farmers' market" but is not exactly. Instead, it is a "food market" that offers a combination of produce, local artisan products, meals, snacks, and just plain tourist stuff. Certainly, the two fish vendors cannot offer anything local and too much of the cheese looks imported. There is enough though—enough to make it a destination for people who want to shop from area farms.

Top: An apple fritter, one of my favorite snacks at Lancaster Central Market
Bottom: The classic building that houses the Lancaster Central Market

There is also a downside to the Lancaster Central Market. On a beautiful day, it keeps you in town and inside which is great if you are in Lancaster City in the first place, but during the harvest season, you may be better off out in the country and choosing your produce from roadside stands. You can save the market for the times you need a roof over your head. It will be there then too.

LANCASTER COUNTY FARMERS MARKET

DELAWARE COUNTY
389 LANCASTER AVE. (ROUTE 30), WAYNE, PA 19087;
LANCASTERCOUNTYFARMERSMARKET.COM; (610) 688-9856

You know how things go. Just when it seems like there is a pattern, a place comes along and breaks it. That is what happened with the Lancaster County Farmers Market; like so many other market houses, it is a beige block of a building on a suburban highway. What is different about this one is that it is on the Main Line in Wayne, one of the most affluent places in the United States. I thought I knew the drill. Pennsylvania indoor market halls were usually in downscale neighborhoods and were a cheap alternative to the chain supermarkets and discount stores the rest of us took for granted.

Here, in an almost window-less structure that (from the outside at least) seems more like a sweatshop than a welcoming outpost of Lancaster County farm country, you will find the most upscale market house that exists. Imagine the Lancaster Central Market (see p. 112) turned up to an eleven. Do parents bring their kids here after a horse show to grab some lunch? Do they send their maids? (At least one vendor assured me that the answer to both questions was "yes.") What could market houses sell if they were able to charge twice as much? Let's take a look.

I tried to walk the market aisle by aisle. It did not work, I would get so excited by some food or another that I would stop, gawk, and then forget which direction I was going in. I would look at the prices, recoil, and then notice that the stuff behind the price tags looked far better than in any other market. Cupcakes had more frosting, roast chickens were juicier, vegetables were brighter, and everything was cleaner. Chinese dumplings glistened in a way you would normally see only in the best restaurants. Actually, the Chinese stall was run by Margret Kuo, a chef and restaurateur with near-celebrity status in the region.

Everything besides the food looked distinctly Pennsylvania market house. The fluorescent lighting, orderly rows of white enamel cooler cases, and terribly out-of-place looking Amish salespeople all told one story, and the fresh ducks, whole roasted racks of pork, and heavily marbled porterhouse steaks spoke of something entirely different.

I mean . . . What would a farmers' market sell if there was a Whole Foods right down the street? What could they offer to a demographic that did not really do that much cooking? I saw macarons, shoofly pie, and biscotti in adjoining cases with a whole cooler devoted to quiche across the way. For this crowd, all were on their radar.

A lot of it was really good. As I strolled from vendor to vendor, my thoughts became a sort of poem:

> looks better
> is better
> costs more
> ouch!

Because I could not afford much, I wanted to leave, but I kept noticing hints of fancy butting up against the general market house mentality—here in Wayne, a butcher boasted "beef, pork, veal, lamb." In the rest of the state, it would say nothing more than "beef and pork," even if a leg of lamb appeared at Easter. I needed to return with a person who held a graduate degree in social class studies. Were there subtle clues I did not even notice?

If it were some fancy store, I would have been turned off. This idea of a superior market house was thrilling though. The prices could have actually been low for the area. The really ritzy shopping mall right behind the market—and invisible from the road— seemed to do a better job of fitting the stereotype of the neighborhood. It was tough to imagine anybody who shopped there visiting a market house afterward.

Even after I got home, I could remember a bone-in pork roast—an eighteen-inch-long solid block of perfectly cooked pork chop being offered for takeout—had anything like this been served anywhere during the past century? Funky and decadent all at once, it looked like it belonged either in a Victorian novel or at the wedding buffet of a *Top Chef* contestant. And yet here it was, available to

The small sign by Route 30 that advertises the Lancaster County Farmers Market in Wayne

anybody who happened to have far more money to spend on a hunk of pork than most of us could ever dream of.

LICKING CREEK BEND FARM

FULTON COUNTY
928 DONAHOE LN., NEEDMORE, PA 17238;
LICKINGCREEKBENDFARM.COM

Michael Tabor is one of those wiry, leathery, spent-his-life-on-the-farm types who clearly looks like he has his share of stories to tell. He was one of those city kids whose connection to the land consisted of his grandmother's tales of the old country and packets of seeds he bought and planted in his school garden in urban Brooklyn. If he were twenty today, he would sound pretty normal, he's deep in his seventies though and that makes you think that if he grew up in the city and spent his whole adult life farming, there must have been communal living somewhere in his past.

And that is the truth. Michael came to Licking Creek Bend Farm in 1972 with a group of folks who described themselves (and their commune) as a "diaspora *kibbutz*." They planted a huge garden, dreamed of a future where they practiced equality and fed the poor, and had their dreams literally blown away when Hurricane Agnes destroyed their crop.

The other *Kibbutzniks* may have left, but Michael stayed. Soon he was growing quality produce and wanted to feed the poor with it. What could he do? His idea was simple; he filled a truck, drove it into a low-income community in Washington, DC and started selling. Urban farmers markets are so common today that it is all too easy to forget how radical an idea this was.

Back in the seventies, the only retail customers for most fresh vegetables were thought to be health food fanatics. Home cooks bought canned or frozen, even at harvest time. To most consumers of the era, the only fresh vegetables they ate at home were iceberg lettuce, celery stalks, and occasional tomato slices. It had not yet occurred to anybody that urban shoppers would flood markets supplied by local farmers.

Licking Creek and its owner are no less radical today; Michael describes it as being "worker-run" with daily meetings. I got an extra dose of Licking Creek idealism when I asked if he grew organically. "Organic is for the wealthy . . . for corporations!" In the neighborhoods he sells in, the word is seen to mean "expensive" or "elite,"

Top left bottom: A distinctive hand-painted truck from Licking Creek Bend Farm standing ready to be loaded with produce for the big city
Top right: The hand-painted mailbox at Licking Creek Bend Farm in Needmore

something that is not for him. The goal is to grow food for people who do not have any real chance of getting it at fancy supermarkets.

Arriving at the farm, the first thing you will notice is a small fleet of box trucks. All are hand-painted with agrarian or vegetable themes in what people today may call a "sixties" or "hippie" style. At least one features an old guy with a big beard on a tractor and another bears the slogan "eat more kale." There is no question that the farm producing what is inside those trucks has counterculture roots, but no claim of the most important fact—this was the farm that pretty much invented downtown markets. When you buy a bunch of carrots from a city farm stand, you have Michael Tabor to thank.

LONGACRE'S MODERN DAIRY BAR

BERKS COUNTY
1445 ROUTE 100, BARTO, PA 19504;
LONGACRESDAIRY.COM; (610) 845-7551

I find it curious that the space in front of the entrance to Longacre's Modern Dairy Bar strongly resembles a bus stop. It has a big awning, park benches, and a few picnic tables too. At any time or season when a person may reasonably want some ice cream, Longacre's is packed with customers, so an area suited to sitting and waiting makes sense.

People also hang around after they have gotten their ice cream: multiple generations of families sharing and swapping flavors and groups of uniformed workers on break intently debating which variety is best. It is a rural, roadside spot, but somehow, Longacre's has managed to re-create a lively urban space from more than half a century ago.

This is the perfect fusion of old and new ice cream cultures, crazy sundaes and hot dogs described on the menu as "pan fried" along with cups of small-batch eccentric flavors. Grab a Graham Slam cone or a cup of Peanut Butter Swirl and eat it at the bus stop. No bus actually stops there though, instead, you just enjoy yourself and your ice cream as if you were about to leave on a big adventure.

This is craft ice cream—the ice cream equivalent of micro-brewing. Perhaps we could call it "micro-churning?" It is made by a small, dedicated group and sold only at the dairy and a few local shops chosen for proximity rather than fanciness. Longacre's ice cream walks a tightrope of tradition vs creativity.

One really has to wonder how Longacre's has managed to hold on to their location on a busy highway between Pottstown and Allentown. Why is it here instead of a fast-food burger restaurant or chain auto parts store? How come it hasn't been torn down? The answer is clear enough—the ice cream here is a deal, good enough to be called great and inexpensive enough for most people to buy. Longacre's is not a luxury; it is just a solid, basic treat that can please almost anybody.

Inside the store, there is wood paneling straight from the fifties and a formica-topped bar with stainless steel syrup pumps that does not seem any newer. The signs that announce the available ice cream

Left: Look for this sign pointing the way to Longacre's Modern Dairy Bar
Right: A basic cup of Longacre's ice cream

flavors have a vintage look too, even when the flavors themselves are more contemporary. There is also a separate, outdoor soft serve window, and finally, the long list of interesting flavors served simply that distinguishes modern, artisan ice cream shops—an idea that may well be retro in itself.

When you are sitting on those benches with your cup of Tin Roof or Cherry Garden, you may want to declare this the best ice cream in the state. Perhaps so when it comes to this classic American style. Pennsylvania is more than that though, always more.

LOST BREAD CO.

PHILADELPHIA COUNTY
1313 N. HOWARD ST., PHILADELPHIA, PA 19122;
LOSTBREADCO.COM; (215) 739-2904

I was not the only writer getting work done at Lost Bread in Philadelphia. All around me, there were notebooks out and laptops powering on. There is plenty to write about here. First of all, it is in South Kensington, a neighborhood that is feeling the heat of gentrification breathing down its neck. And then there is the food they serve: bread, a few pastries, and at a separate counter, coffee. We cannot be more than a fifteen-minute walk from La Colombe (see p. 105) and even though both are in re-purposed industrial buildings; they could not offer more different atmospheres.

Lost Bread is not chic, but it is also permeated with a fear of it. You can sit here, order some toast and butter, and not feel like you are in the wrong place. So that is what I did. I got myself some buttered toast sprinkled with coarse salt and a shot of espresso. The toast came on a steel tray and the coffee in a glass. Cool and modest at the same time.

I bit into a thick slice and the flavor of real bread stepped out to meet me like an old friend. After visiting a few bakeries, I was coming to expect deliciousness in round, sourdough loaves, but I still was not prepared for toast. These slices of lightly browned, rectangular white bread looked commercial enough, but they were filled with resounding flavor. Real bread! It could be in any shape! No matter how you eat it, there were better possibilities.

Next was a bran muffin. It tasted of bran and made the bran seem worth eating. Most bran muffins taste of sugar, nuts, seeds, and raisins. The idea is simple; bran is supposed to be really good for you so bakers buy the cheapest, most tasteless bran they can find and doll it up. Not here. Here, the bran itself delivers. This is the idea—foods made from grain that taste like they are made from the best grain you can imagine. Not tasteless, not sugary, not smothered with dried fruit or olives.

On the shelf behind the counter were loaves with names that reminded me of local beers, "buck honey rye," "milk bread," "whole wheat redeemer," and "homadama." All had dark crusts and the aura of earnestness that the best breads emit. They were all there without affectation. The plain steel shelves sat on plain concrete floors. The folks behind the counter acted like they really knew their stuff.

Lost Bread is itself more than anything else. It is urban with a nod toward the farmers who provide its ingredients. Lots of folks would expect a product like this to come from a farm shop, others would think that loaves like these would have be astronomically priced and sold in the most expensive city neighborhoods. Lost Bread will disappoint all of them. Here you get a very well-made product, a reasonable price, and a place to sit and eat without the slightest trace of pretense. It is a pretty good deal in my opinion.

Warning—Lost Bread shares this space with Blind Tiger Coffee. You can order both and enjoy them right there, but you will have to leave separate tips for each.

MARCIA'S CHOCOLATES

BLAIR COUNTY
122 GREENWOOD RD., ALTOONA, PA 16602;
MARCIASCHOCOLATES.COM; (814) 201-2504

Even though my GPS insisted I would find the place, I could not believe I was at MarCia's, a modest chocolate maker in Altoona. The building had the look of a rural doctor's office. There was no storefront and only the smallest of signs. Of course, in a place like Altoona, big signs are not really needed. Everybody who wanted to buy quality chocolate in a city the size of Altoona undoubtedly knew where to go.

It was a few days before Valentine's Day and I expected craziness. Of course, Altoona does not do craziness. Instead, there were beautiful chocolate rose lollipops, bags of chocolate-covered nuts, fine marshmallows, and a few cases of (chocolate) truffles.

Look closely at their product. It is not slick mass-produced supermarket chocolate, and it is not snooty or elegant either. Instead, each piece has a sort of homemade roughness to it, as if your grandma—or maybe MarCia's grandma—made it especially for you. MarCia's Chocolate is a mid-priced missing link that sits above the industrial stuff in quality and below the single-origin chocolates in price.

MarCia's Chocolates have the look of the best homemade candy

At the display case, the assortment boxes were empty. You are offered two choices: a fifteen- or thirty-piece box, and best of all, you can choose what goes in. It can be anything from peanut clusters to chocolate sea-salted caramel. If you are giving a gift to an obsessive, fill the box with only one kind. Otherwise, choose from what is out there. Three or four of each will fill the big one.

MarCia grew up in Portage, a smaller town nearby, where her grandma taught her how to make chocolates. Grandma was not an old-world crafter; she took a class in the late seventies, dove right in, and mastered the art with the young MarCia (still called "Marcia" in those days) by her side.

As MarCia grew up, she set aside chocolate and earned a doctorate in physical therapy, served twenty-five years in the military doing just that, and then returned to Altoona. Back in town, she continued her chocolate making as a hobby. As many passionate craftspeople will tell you, doing your passion as a hobby is not really enough. And that is when MarCia's Chocolates was born.

Well not exactly . . . there is also the matter of that doctor's office building. It turns out that part of the motivation for transitioning from hobby to business was the building—a former holistic health center as it turns out—owned by her husband. And with the skills and the space, a professional chocolate maker was born.

She has been at it for three "seasons." "Seasons" because they close in summer when the collective Pennsylvania appetite turns to ice cream. Otherwise, she is there, a charming and energetic figure with a store full of chocolate and a readiness to pack up a box for you.

It was almost Valentine's Day and I joined the crowed in buying a few chocolate roses. At two dollars each, they were a nice gift without being extravagant. Later that same evening, I handed one to my wife as a sort of pre–Valentine's Day gift. It struck just the right note.

MASSER'S FARM MARKET

NORTHUMBERLAND COUNTY
6148 STATE ROUTE 61; PAXINOS, PA 17860;
MASSERSFARMMARKET.COM; (570) 644-1377

What is it about coal country and meat? Masser's Farm Market is yet another rural butcher shop that forces the question. The location could be a set for a heartbreak movie in Appalachia. It is tucked under a hillside railroad line with heaps of anthracite just down the road. Like everything else in these parts, there are more questions than answers. There is no farm, but there is a market and a smokehouse. Most of all, it is an island of comfort food in a place that has seen more than its share of pain.

Drive up, get out of your car, and inhale deeply. There is that special aroma of smoke and pork that defines the region. Spend some time in coal country and you will learn that smokehouses are a truly welcome sight. A place where foods that are both delicious and traditional are being made by your friends and neighbors.

Once you are inside, you will see that Masser's does not hide anything. There is a case of fresh beef and pork, a couple of cases of sausages, and a cooler in the back with some amazing looking hams. I stared at first, and then tried to take some pictures. Those hams

A bunch of whole smoked hams on display at Masser's Market

were not dry country hams, and they were not industrially processed either. They were just the way Pennsylvania hams were a century ago. You could buy them whole, in parts, or sliced into steaks.

I thought those hams were the stars of the show until I saw the ring bologna. There were lots of them stacked up in a cooler case. Not for long though. People were buying them like crazy. According to the food traditions of Pennsylvania, you could snack on them, slice them for sandwiches, cook chunks of them in stews, or even pickle them in jars.

There was prepared food to go too; creamed cucumber salad, pepper cabbage, ham pot pie, and ham and bean soup, they all seemed Pennsylvania Dutch. So did the pickles. Did the Pennsylvania Dutch go to the mountains and work in the mines? Or maybe they came to cook for the miners.

A sign on the wall offered "faggots," and when I asked about them, the guy behind the counter seemed to be sincerely unaware that it was the British word for "meatballs." I imagined miners just off the boat from Wales or Northumberland (we were in Northumberland County after all) seeking a touch of home, never dreaming their foods would be remembered a hundred and fifty years later.

Masser's is yet another one of those places you want to tell people to visit. It is just that you cannot imagine why anybody who did not know it would be in that part of Pennsylvania in the first place. If you have reason to be in or around Shamokin and have an interest in food, you have certainly already heard about it. Otherwise, it is not near any big highways or universities, the typical visitor draws of the region, but maybe, just maybe, that is its appeal.

The foods folks are eating in coal country may have roots in Europe; British, Italian, Polish, and German too, but now—after 150 years or so—it had all become Pennsylvanian.

MEADVILLE MARKET HOUSE

CRAWFORD COUNTY
910 MARKET ST., MEADVILLE, PA 16335;
MEADVILLEMARKETHOUSE.ORG; (814) 336-2056

The Meadville Market House is a small-town indoor market, something we associate with eastern, agricultural Pennsylvania. It is less than thirty miles from the Ohio line and close to Erie—pretty much as far west as you can go without being in a whole different state. It is in Meadville, a town that looks like it should be in Illinois or Indiana, rather than Pennsylvania. Surrounded by twentieth-century buildings and set in a grid of urban streets, you will find it—an old structure that looks for all the world like a Victorian-era train station—right on Market Street. Here you can find locally produced meats, cheeses, canned items, and seasonal produce too.

Just by looking around, you can imagine the struggle American towns this size have experienced. Today, the decay has stopped and new businesses are stepping in. Clothing, restaurants, renovated banks, and professional offices fill the neighborhood again. It is a comeback for the town and a comeback for the market too.

The Meadville Market House has another claim to fame; it is the oldest continuously operating market building in the state. Opened in 1870, it hasn't ceased operations since. This does not mean it is the oldest market, farmers in Easton (see p. 62) have been gathering and selling on the same spot since 1752, and while Lancaster's Central Market (see p. 112) has been operating in one form or another since 1730, its present building was opened in 1889.

Check out some old photos. It is an island that stays still while everything around it changes. Through the years, the streets got paved, the buildings around it transformed from wood country homes to urban brick, and parking meters found their way to the Market House's perimeter. The structure, with its awnings that resemble train station platforms, has remained still, somehow a monument and a working business all at once.

When edge-of-town supermarkets started taking root in the fifties, the Market House seemed to be sliding downhill. By the seventies, the town wanted to demolish it, and while that did not happen, it was nothing more than a flea market for the next few decades. The

Market House needed somebody to save it and a new arrival in town, Alice Sjolander, turned out to be the right person for the task.

Raised in Philadelphia and a lifelong fan of farmers' markets, she found herself in Meadville thanks to her husband's job. The town needed the market, but local farmers were not quite ready to take the leap. As Alice saw it, "Farmers needed a place to market their goods, and people did not want their family farms to become museums."

Back in 2005, farmers' markets were not a normal sight in towns like Meadville. Although they were thriving in New York, Philadelphia, and Washington, DC, small mid-western industrial towns had not yet gotten the word . . . or maybe they'd seen those city markets on television and decided it was not for them—the root of the "museum" comments, I think.

It has come a long way since Alice started. Today you will find about forty vendors of artisan foods and crafts year-round and in season, an outdoor farmers' market at the same spot. The Meadville Market House has now returned to being what it was long ago; a place where local people gather, shop, and share. Indeed, Alice told me, "The Market House is smiling, her children are coming back again."

After all this time, Alice has become "The Grand Dame of the Market." Why? Well, the market may have forty vendors, but it has only one cashier: Alice herself. She keeps a sharp eye on things.

A shrine for deceased relatives during the Day of the Dead in Kennett Square

MEXICAN IN KENNETT SQUARE

CHESTER COUNTY

HNOS. LARA, 710 W. BALTIMORE PIKE, KENNETT SQUARE, PA 19348; HNOSLARA.COM; (610) 925-3349

LA PENA MEXICANA TAQUERIA, 609 W. CYPRESS ST., KENNETT SQUARE, PA 19348; (610) 925 2651

A RINCONSITO ROSTICERIA Y TORTILLERIA, 717 W. CYPRESS ST. KENNETT SQUARE, PA 19348; (610) 444-2274

A group of little boys were staring at me and I was not enjoying it. I had ordered the unspeakable and their dad had just explained it to them. Nobody knew me, nobody knew anything about me except one thing—I had just requested a plate of tacos filled with cow tongue. Being suburban kids, they had to see it. They watched *Bizzare Foods* on television and they'd certainly been told that Mexican food in Kennett Square was a great eating adventure, now I was inadvertently demonstrating just how great an adventure it was. Was I about to eat the same stuff as those guys on television? Would I die from it? There was fear in the air.

It was another day in Kennett Square, Pennsylvania's best destination for authentic Mexican food. I worry about the place. I worry that the head, tongue, and tripe tacos will disappear in a miasma of squealing and groaning. And I fear that someday, I will stroll into one of those Mexican storefronts—the kinds of restaurants that people love to call "joints," and find nothing but burritos, chips, and salsa.

What has happened to Kennett Square? This used to be a quiet town of mushroom farmers after all. Today, there are trappings of wealth with fine-dining restaurants and boutiques lining the streets. It is still surrounded by mushroom farms, but the elegance of neighboring towns like Chadd's Ford and Hockessin has left a mark. That is all well and good, but if you are wondering why you should visit, the reason will have nothing to do with either. Instead, head on over because Kennett Square has the best Mexican shops and restaurants for miles in any direction.

You can visit Kennett Square any time, there are at least a few Mexican places that open at six in the morning and/or do not close

The sign welcomes you to La Pena Mexicana Taqueria in Kennett Square

until after ten at night. However, if you can only come on one day, make it The Day of The Dead. This is when the town comes together for some serious celebration with shrines, workshops in holiday traditions, a parade, and special foods.

The shrines are memorials to lost loved ones and display what they cherished the most. Food is almost always front and center. The deceased are honored here with the simplest meals imaginable. The emotions you see in these displays of tamales, fast-food fries, or even cans of Spam can overwhelm you. It is food for the dead and the living too. Sometimes a tamale is nothing more than a quick snack, yet here, it is a metaphor for a whole person. It is a resounding reminder that a love of food is a love of life itself.

On other days, head down to Cypress Street. There you will find a bunch of small restaurants and an impressive grocery store. At La Pena Mexicana Taqueria, an order-at-the-counter sort of place with warm red and yellow walls, I asked for hurraches. Ordering it bestowed instant respect upon me. The eyes of all three people behind the counter said, "This guy knows what is good."

In La Pena, there were plenty of reasons to cry. The mixture of homesickness, passion, skill, and hospitality that makes a modest place like this thrive is cemented with tears. Nobody would put this sort of effort into what is essentially a snack bar unless they are possessed with the soul of a cook and a love for whomever may be eating there. Sit and listen to the sound of the kitchen. No screaming, no soundtrack; just chopping, grilling, pouring, and stirring. A gastronomic symphony. I could feel the humanity in every bite. Was the crew in the kitchen even conscious of this? Do you have to think about it if your craft says it for you?

Hnos. Lara is the name of a Mexican grocery down the street that dishes a pretty big helping of homesickness itself. Yes, if you are the sort of gringo that I am, the vast array of tortillas will sternly whisper "If you do not know what we are all for, you do not belong here." That is just the beginning of the mystery though. There are dozens of items

I had never seen outside of Mexico, and if you need a snack, you will find a fridge filled with beautiful *gelatinas*—those layered desserts that too many Mexican/American restaurants forget about.

At La Rinconsito Rosticeria y Tortelleria, a pregnant woman ate alone, the empty seats around her offering up another helping of the homesickness that permeates Mexican Kennett Square. Here, a tray was brought out to me with a basket of tortilla chips, but instead of the typical salsas, there was a creamy red cabbage salad and a searing yellow hot sauce. Their menu listed the expected: tacos and *tortas* with both the typical fillings and a few more ambitious dishes with flank steak or grilled shrimp.

I tried to imagine somebody who came to Pennsylvania from Mexico missing their food. It could

A street sign advertising Day of the Dead activities in Kennett Square

have been anybody; a college student, a grandma, a young family . . . anybody . . . and then they came down here to Cypress Street and found this very passionate homage to their cuisine. They would certainly be homesick, and very happy too.

MISTER ED'S ELEPHANT MUSEUM & CANDY EMPORIUM

ADAMS COUNTY
6019 CHAMBERSBURG RD., ORRTANNA, PA 17353;
MISTEREDS.COM; (717) 352-3792

If you are the sort of person who has to ask if Mister Ed's Elephant Museum & Candy Emporium is a tourist trap, you are most certainly missing the point. It is on the old Lincoln Highway, a road that has seen more than a few tourist attractions in its time. It fits into the genre with a patch of huge plastic and cement elephants and a roadside candy store. It cannot really be anything else, can it?

You'd be better off asking if it is a tourist trap that is worth a visit. The answer to that one is a resounding, "Yes." Stopping here, at this remote spot west of Gettysburg is just plain fun and not very expensive at all. The elephant statues—arranged in gardens and identified with cute signs—are worth a moment of your time. The shop with its candy, snacks, elephant souvenirs, and clean restrooms seals the deal.

Pull over and take a stroll. Check out the gardens and then go inside. There is a lot of candy. So much that kids are jumping up and down before they even go through the door. Just the thought of it is enough. There is more for adults though. A room filled with Pez products seems more like it is for collectors than snackers.

It is the same with a list of other brands associated with nostalgic brands. Swedish Fish, Airheads, Wacky Wafers, Jujyfruits, Milk Duds, and Charleston Chews are all here and crying out to nostalgic grown-ups. All these things add up to a destination that is as much for serious collectors as it is for people who just want some candy.

If you were only offering up sweet snacks for passing travelers, why would they stop at your shop instead of one of those big chain convenience stores? If it is just to buy peanuts and candy bars then there is no reason at all. If you add statues of elephants, a garden to rest in, and a whole host of candies that no chain sells, a stop becomes more compelling.

There is plenty to snack on. Bags of nuts and pretzels sit alongside not only every sort of candy you know, but quite a few that you do not. And then there is fudge. Clearly, there are people out there who love the stuff. While I was at Mister Ed's, there were customers discussing fudge in the way some others describe wine.

Because I have never been a fudge fan, I went with something I have loved for decades—a chocolate-covered pretzel. It was a perfect snack to get me back on Route 30 and through the vast jam of Gettysburg.

In order to be a perfect stop, Mister Ed's would need something to drink alongside all that sugar. A modest coffee and tea bar for the adults, and some milk for the kids would round it out nicely. But then, it would be more modern rest stop than classic tourist attraction, and I am not sure that would be a good move.

What is most amazing about Mister Ed's though is what they have achieved with only a tiny fraction of the money the big theme parks spend—the ability to use animal statues and candy to make large numbers of people crack a smile. The elephants will warm your heart, the collectibles will charm you, and a few candies or a fistful of nuts will give you the energy to face Route 30, the old Lincoln Highway, and finish the next leg of your trip.

Note—Do not get the wrong impression, there are no live elephants here.

Top: The storefront at Mister Ed's
Middle and bottom: The grounds of
Mister Ed's are home to elephant
statues like these two

Mister Ed's Elephant Museum & Candy Emporium   133

MISTY CREEK GOAT DAIRY

LANCASTER COUNTY
43 W. EBY RD., LEOLA, PA 17540;
MISTYCREEKGOATDAIRY.NET; (717) 656-4628

There is a dream some of us have. In it, we're driving on a quiet country road and turn down a pastoral farm lane. On one side, there is a tiny schoolhouse with Amish children playing softball, on the other, fields being cultivated by a mule team. Soon, there is a barn behind a huge stack of hay bales. You park there, spend a few moments playing with the happy animals, and then head into the farm shop. There, artisan cheeses that would be considered excellent by any global standard are being sold by a cheerful Amish man surrounded by his utterly adorable children. For some of us, this is a fantasy. For a lucky few, this is reality at Misty Creek Goat Dairy.

Before we go over the top in pastoral reverie, let's get one thing straight—there is absolutely no tradition of Amish farmers making aged cheeses in Pennsylvania. You won't find a recipe in any historic cookbook or instructions in one of the many older farming manuals that fill Lancaster County libraries. The handful of Amish and Mennonite farmers making these cheeses today began in the last twenty-five years.

The owner and cheese maker at Misty Creek is Amos G. Miller. While he took the temperature of a huge steel vat of milk, Amos told me, "This is just starting . . . it is a whole new wave. Only one person in

The home of Misty Creek's dairy goats

the county is a second-generation cheese maker." He went on to say, "We Amish live in a vacuum. We do not travel to Europe . . . and now, we're getting out of that vacuum."

Early on, Amos realized he wanted to make cheese. He had a good start. He was milking goats, earning some money, and the skill and craft of cheese were beckoning.

There was a lot to learn. Back then, he'd go visit his brother in Wisconsin and seek out the local cheeses. In the beginning, he'd go for the cheapest stuff he could find, and as the years passed, he'd set his sights higher and higher until he only sought out the finest products. Finally, he reached a point where he not only knew the best; he was able to make his own.

Amos seeks out bleu cheeses. (Not "blue," please!) He loves both eating them and making them. My own favorite of his is Mist o' Bleu, a sharp, salty, all-goat product with a parchment color punctuated by turquoise veins. He has milder bleu varieties too, although purists will go for the Mist.

It is just one corner of his vast range. Besides the bleus, there are cheddars made from goat milk, soft fresh cheeses more like French chèvre, and his takes on popular styles like Munster and Swiss. There is even more though; he uses his formidable cheese-making skill to produce products for neighbors too. Even so, it is a one-man (plus his children) operation. Indeed, soon those children will become a Misty Creek second generation.

One day, while we were talking about Amish foodways, Miller told me, "I do not appreciate my cheese being called Amish. I think it is wrong. Rather, I want it sold for what it is." This is an important point. Many of us see visiting Lancaster County Amish farms as a special treat. We're still equating their faith and image with a high degree of artisanship. And yet, for the Amish farmer we're visiting, it is something of an excuse. He wants us to come because his cheese is special, not because of his religion or how he dresses his children.

I am both a tourist and a cheese lover. The agrarian back roads of Lancaster County are a pleasure to visit unto themselves and the pious farm families who line those roads with local, artisan foods are among Pennsylvania's great treasures. Once you start appreciating their products, their craft takes center stage and their religion fades into the background. I visit Misty Creek for the cheese.

NECESSITY FARMS & DAIRY

MONTGOMERY COUNTY
202 GREEN HILL RD., TELFORD, PA 18969;
NECESSITYFARMS.COM; (267) 382-0556

When you drive up to Necessity Farms & Dairy in Telford, you get the feeling of country for a few minutes, and when you park in the farm shop lot, there is a wonderful sense of the pastoral about the place. This is almost, although not quite, a fantasy. The grazing animals, the fields of grass, and the agrarian atmosphere that envelops you, will leave you thinking you are in a very rural place. It is not really. It is a short hop from a couple of major highways and an easy drive from Allentown, Philadelphia, and large swaths of densely populated New Jersey. For people who want to buy meats and poultry on the farm, this is an easy trip.

Necessity Farms covers thirty-two acres. Small by statewide standards and big enough—as owners Steve and Carol Branning remind us—for a lot of work. Sheep are their strength, and then there are goats, cattle, chickens, ducks, and rabbits too. Combine that with a commercial kitchen that uses their own products to make soups and broths and you have a pretty solid farm-based food business. As for "dairy," it is part of the name because the former owner used the property to produce cheeses; Steve and Carol haven't done any commercial milking in years.

Because Necessity Farms is so close to heavily populated areas and depends on retail sales for revenue, it has to cater to a wide range of tastes. Those prepared soups are great for people in a hurry, while simple cuts of beef and chicken work for casual meals. More esoteric items like bone-in roasts go to serious cooks.

Big-city immigrant food markets and restaurants were the main customers for sheep, goat, duck, and rabbit. The Covid pandemic has changed things a bit, duck has suddenly become a favorite with home cooks who wanted something a bit different than chicken, and so has rabbit. Not just for cooking though. It turns out that people were buying rabbits as pets too. My only experience with this was the "pets or meat" scene from the film *Roger and Me*. And as usual, I was wrong. Rabbits can be litterbox trained and apparently do well in suburban homes.

Steve and his wife Carol are using the former dairy area for aquaponics, the craft of raising fish and plants in the same environment. They began with trout and that did not quite work out. Trout are sensitive to many of the factors that are tough to control on a small farm. So now they are trying tilapia, a fish with a better ability to survive. Tilapia gets a bad rap because so much of what we see is raised on farms with conditions that are most politely described as disappointing. Kept in a clean space and fed properly, the results can be promising, and hopefully, we will find out sooner rather than later.

Necessity is one of Pennsylvania's officially preserved farms. This does not mean it is public or a museum of some sort. Instead, this is a legal guarantee that it won't be sold for any use except agriculture. Given that this farm is awfully close to serious development of every sort, a bit of preserved green is welcome.

That being said, the farm is a very real part of a varied community. Steve's tales of farm life are co-mingled with his experiences as a local citizen. His explanation of the problems he faced in trout farming somehow also got combined with the story of how he rescued a school bus stranded in a blizzard. The legend of the theft of their tomato cages blended smoothly with Carol's gratitude for how neighbors and customers chipped in to help them get new ones.

There is something about a name like Necessity Farms that made me think that it was very old. I was hoping it dated back to the colonial era and it did not. When Steve and Carol first bought the place in 2013, they kept the previous owner's name for a year, but as they settled in, it no longer seemed to fit. They kept finding that the farm needed more and whenever they improvised a solution, one would declare, "Necessity is the mother of invention." It seemed like the farm had a whole lot of necessities, and a name was born.

THE NESTING BOX MARKET AND CREAMERY

BERKS COUNTY
230 SNYDER RD., KEMPTON, PA 19529;
(760) 981-9518

Not many farms in Pennsylvania feel as rural and remote as The Nesting Box. Even though it is only a couple of miles from I-78, there are few places that appear more isolated. All you see from the front porch are the family farm, some patches of woods, and the narrow one-lane road that leads there. That is Snyder Road—it is a real road, not a driveway. The Nesting Box and the family farm it is attached to are the only buildings along it for a very long way. After the corn is harvested and views stretch across to the horizon, it is just ground and sky.

When you've gone a bit farther down Snyder than you would expect to, you will see the shop, right there in front of you and oozing enough charm to melt anybody's heart. You can always tell when it is open because a crowd will gather moments after the door is unlocked. They are not neighbors—there are not any neighbors. It is a lot of people from Kutztown, Allentown, or Reading who have sought the place out.

With a name like The Nesting Box, you would think the farm shop would be chicken and egg focused. And with the word "creamery" in its name, you may suspect that cows may somehow be involved. Not exactly. It is on a farm with chickens and a couple of hundred acres of crops too, but in this—one of the most beautiful farm shops in the state—you will not find any chicken. Well . . . there are not any cows either. "Creamery" is a reference to the ice cream scoop shop that occupies about a quarter of the

Top: You know you're in dairy country when you see messages like this one painted on bales of hay Locals call them "baleboards"
Bottom: A tiny sign by the side of the road points the way to The Nesting Box

The view from The Nesting Box parking lot; this is perhaps the most solitary setting for a retail shop in this book

store. They make ice cream there even though they do not milk the cows.

There is a pretty good selection of Berks County artisan foods. They produce enough eggs on the farm for the shop, a few other stores, and some restaurants. They have far more than eggs though. Jams, syrups, preserves, and honey from Funny Farm Apiary (see p. 71) too. More of a surprise were artisan frozen pizzas (how often do you see that?) and frozen goat cheese pierogies too. Locally made cheeses and yogurts round off the selection in the off season.

I felt restless at The Nesting Box. I wanted a sack of yellow potatoes and I wanted to talk to Timi, the owner too. She appeared to feel much the same way; happy to answer questions and even happier to sell me those potatoes—the last remaining local produce. When I told her how remote the place felt, her response was a succinct, "That is what a farm is." I could only wish this was always true. So many farms were edged with suburban homes, strip malls, and professional offices that I doubted her claim.

Come here and stand on the porch, this farm is remote, isolated, and really quiet. It is a definition of rural that has almost vanished. The view is of the empty. Study it. If the weather is on your side, have an ice cream while you ponder. You are just a few minutes from the highway and maybe a few minutes more to a nice college town, and yet, it is still somehow nowhere.

NEW EASTERN MARKET

YORK COUNTY
201 MEMORY LN., YORK, PA 17402;
NEWEASTERNMARKET.COM; (717) 755-5811

It did not take any specialized demographic research to see that New Eastern Market in York was more popular than any neighboring supermarket. After all, the sheer number of cars in the parking lot told most of the story. While the chains had only a smattering, New Eastern was packed to the point you had to wait in line for a space to become available. Inside, you could tell that every one of those cars brought people who came for serious shopping.

Unlike most of the other market houses in this book, New Eastern Market is an easy drive from at least three others and yet, it pulls off its uniqueness effortlessly. While the markets in Lancaster County or downtown York hurl headfirst into the food court and tourism industries, New Eastern Market thrives as a time machine. If you want to know what those other markets were like thirty years ago, this is where you have to come.

The name has some history. York has had a market on the east side of town for a very long time, just not in the same place. Fire destroyed the previous one in the late forties and this building was purpose-built to replace it. Hence the "New" in the name.

I first stumbled upon the time warp when I visited the cooked-food vendors in the back row. There I found deep-fried chicken livers. First, I stared, then I remembered Grandpa eating them outdoors somewhere . . . maybe Coney Island? Was it in 1963? Mine were pretty good, but they could have used a nice sea breeze to bring them over the top. No breeze came, but there was a bottle of cream soda to wash it down with—Grandpa's favorite! Without question, this was the least healthy meal I had eaten in all those years and I was reveling in it. This was not junk food; it was from before the era of junk food.

Here are the pan puddings, smoked sausages, heaps of shredded dried beef, and mayonnaise-laden salads that had gone missing from Amish country as it gentrified at warp speed. Outdoors, it may have been peak season for zucchini flowers, but you wouldn't dare ask for them here. You cannot help but notice an edge of deliberate scruffiness in the crowd. Their appearance says, "We know about all that trendy stuff, but we do not do it, we're in York."

There it all was, what people in central Pennsylvania cooked and ate before the first fast-food restaurant or chain supermarket opened. For the most part, you have to be a formidable home cook to appreciate what is on offer here; roasts, cured pork products, and fresh vegetables are the bulk of it and the customers were scrutinizing every last morsel. This can only leave you asking who shops here, who crowds that parking lot? How did they manage to miss fast food and frozen dinners and somehow retain the skills to cook these ingredients?

Do the rest of us have it all wrong? Maybe this was what the American food revolution was really supposed to be about. The vendors at New Eastern Market are real farmers and artisans and the customers are real home cooks. While the rest of us were visiting the restaurants of "visionary" food celebrities, there were people shopping at New Eastern Market—jamming its parking lot so they could buy the reasonably priced and locally produced food those visionaries were dreaming of . . . and maybe snacking on a few fried chicken livers while they shopped.

Foods to Look For: Pizza

Just what is pizza? Most of us eat it often, and yet it varies so much that we need a working definition. Here's mine—pizza is a flat layer of bread dough covered with tomato sauce and baked until it is cooked through. There is almost always cheese and often something else too; anything from little meatballs to pieces of pineapple. Most people over the age of six or seven have their own favorite pizza toppings; they also have toppings they passionately hate.

A school of Pennsylvania pizza would have a lot to teach. First there is the vocabulary. "Slices" are wedges cut from a disc of round pizza. That could mean big and New York style or the smaller round "pies" that are found everywhere in the world. "Cuts" are rectangular pieces that are taken from a big pan called a "tray." These four words, "slices," "pies," "cuts," and "trays," are the basics of the Pennsylvania pizza vocabulary. Round and square tell you an awful lot about what pizza is going to be put in front of you.

A cut of double crust white pizza at Acraro and Genell

After vocabulary, there is history. The Italian/American food cultures of Old Forge and Philadelphia created pies that were entirely different from each other. Old Forge had its rectangular cuts and drier cheeses, and Philadelphia had its round pies that were as close to Italian as a Pennsylvanian could get at the time. More recently, bigger pies from New York and authentic pizzas that copy what you get in modern Italy have become popular too.

It all breaks down to four genres. First, the round pies made by the chains and copied by more conservative independents, then the trays and cuts that began in Old Forge and are sometimes called "coal country style" (see p. 158), after that you will find "New York" or "Brooklyn" style—really large round pies cut into slices, and finally, the new kid on the block—pizzas that are "authentic." That is, they attempt to replicate the pies served in Italy today. They are smaller, use a moister cheese, and are cooked very quickly in hot—often wood burning—ovens. Even so, there are pizzas from places like Pittsburgh's Beto's (see p. 21) that are unique enough that they defy our basic categories— even if they share something with pizza in other states.

Of course, this will make some of you ask why a copy of something from Italy is "authentic" and an equally accurate copy of something from New York City less so? I mean . . . some of those pizza styles were created a very long time ago and have taken root in their own right. If you find a place that serves "authentic" Old Forge pizza (see p. 144) a couple of hundred miles from Old Forge and they get it right, they are as authentic as any other authentic pizza.

Find your favorite, use the right vocabulary to describe it, and enjoy it without any further analysis.

OLD FORGE: THE PIZZA CAPITAL OF THE WORLD

LACKAWANNA COUNTY
ARCARO & GENELL, 443 S. MAIN ST., OLD FORGE, PA 18518; ARCAROANDGENELL.COM; (570) 457-5555

SALERNO'S CAFE, 139 MOOSIC RD., OLD FORGE, PA 18518; (570) 457-2117

I was in the dining room at Salerno's Cafe in Old Forge, sitting with my wife Maria, and studying the menu. She was in her usual state of Italian-food-induced emotional turmoil and I was deep in a funk that I was starting to call "Pennsylvania culinary bafflement." The menu listed something called "short orders" and the first thing I noticed on the short order list was "tripe." I had visited the area enough times to know that this was small strips of cow stomach simmered in a light tomato sauce. The next item threw me for a loop; it was "soffrito." Having bought more than a few jars of the supermarket stuff, I thought I knew it . . . I just did not understand how they served it. The waitress said, "Ya know . . . soffrito . . . chopped pork hearts . . . do ya not know?"

Nope. I do not think that one person in a thousand outside Old Forge, associates soffrito and pork hearts. I had to have it. And when I tasted it, what I got was the powerful pork flavor that meat from the entire animal once had. The regular cuts of commercially produced pork that we normally eat today are so mild that we've forgotten the pleasures of meat eating. Salerno's soffrito was an introduction to pork as it has been enjoyed for millennia. So, while a family across the dining room worked on a tray of pizza, we went on to the rest of the menu; Maria ordering pasta with a red sausage sauce and I the strange pork heart soffrito.

What was happening? This place was a time machine! I was eating a dish that no restaurant in the rest of the state would consider offering and they did not even make a big deal about it. I shared the love of offal that so many Italians—and so few Americans—display and did not know what to do besides eating it when I could. Our meal was intense, delicious, and a lesson in Pennsylvania Italian culinary history.

Salerno's was not the only place in Old Forge. Arcaro & Genell was a few hundred yards away, and even so, I lost track of the restaurants

A bowl of polenta at Acaro and Genell in Old Forge

that lay in between. A spot in Old Forge had to be good just to exist, right? Both had been there for a very long time.

I ate at Arcaro & Genell a few months later. Pizzas, some with one layer of crust and others with more, filled a large part of the menu. There were "short orders" here too. They did not have pork hearts, although you could find tripe. It was clearly the regional specialty. None of that prepared me for polenta, "porketta," or "tuna fish sauce." How can this be? In a state filled with awful small-town Italian restaurants, I was presented with a serious and truly authentic menu.

Polenta was an automatic choice. For those of you who do not know, it is a hot cereal-like paste of cooked cornmeal usually topped with a sausage-laden red sauce. Arcaro & Genell offered theirs with sausage and mushrooms. I went for it.

And that is where the problem was—Old Forge may claim pizza fame, yet you can order almost anything and expect it to be better than the pizza. Even so, the menu described a wide variety of pizzas, and all were made on rectangular trays and offered in "cuts" rather than slices. Calling them "slices" told the locals you were from New Jersey or worse. I ordered a cut of double-crust white with spinach for the sake of science though.

My polenta and pizza came at the same time. The bowl of polenta was loaded with flavor and smothered in a sauce with even more flavor. It was a dish that fed generations of coal miners. A woman waiting for a table watched me eat it. She leaned over and told me her mother made polenta and served it to her on a wooden board. This is the way serious polenta fanatics do it in Italy, so I asked her where her mother was from. "Old Forge! Right here!" The boundary between Italian and Italian/American is fuzzier than you may think.

I wanted to ask her, "Was it this good?" But I did not. Instead, I asked if she put butter on it along with the tomato sauce the way they do in Italian mountain huts. She recoiled; her mom must have been from olive oil country.

And the pizza? Two layers of flatbread with melted cheese and cooked spinach between them. If this were a hip, big city grilled cheese shack, I would have pronounced it fantastic. It did not hold a candle to that bowl of polenta though. It was a nice novelty facing off against a few hundred years of well-executed Italian culinary tradition. Two serious contenders, but not a fair fight.

There are questions about my Old Forge meals that an Italian cuisine purist may ask, but at that moment, I was not a purist. I was so full of polenta and sauce that I could not even finish the contents of my bread basket—a food waste crime if there ever was one. I was stupefied.

ORAM'S DONUT SHOP

BEAVER COUNTY
1406 SEVENTH AVE., BEAVER FALLS, PA 15010;
ORAMS.COM; (724) 846-1504

What sort of shop would you expect to see on the main street of an old Pennsylvania river town? Tile storefront? Stainless trim? Screen door? That is Oram's. It is old-school perfect. Inside, it is all donuts, all the time. No counter, no seats. You go in, get your donuts and leave. It is possible to have a conversation here if—and this is an important if—the topic is donuts.

I stood in line and the guy in front of me noticed I was not a regular. "This is the epicenter of the donut universe," he said to me as if I did not already know. I wanted to say something like, "Come on dude! Why else would anybody come here?" and did not. He followed up with, "Have you read my online reviews?" I bluffed. Oram's has lots of online reviews to read and I had only tackled a few.

Having a business that specializes in doing a really good job of making something that everybody likes is smart, and Oram's does it right. There are filled donuts covered with chocolate frosting or powdered sugar and regular donut-shaped donuts too. There are enough varieties to feel like you have a choice and not so many that it starts seeming like a gimmick.

Their most basic seemed to be custard-filled and powdered. It was perfect to look at. Palm-sized, and the right amount of sugar too. After a few bites, I decided that the taste lived up to its reputation. Okay, the custard was not made from local, raw eggs, but it did not have the strange aftertaste you find all-to-often in independent donut shops.

A donut from Oram's

I also tried something a bit more exotic—a banana-cream-filled donut with chocolate frosting. This was a bit more thought-provoking. There was no fresh banana, just a cream that was slightly more

The sign welcoming you to Oram's Donut Shop in Beaver Falls

yellow than the basic custard. As for the chocolate, it was good quality frosting with a few yellow sprinkles on top. I assume they were there to remind the bakers of what they put inside.

As I leaned against my car and finished off my donuts, I understood. This was not the perfect donut shop; it was the donut perfectionist's shop. What was served here was the traditional thing, the classic American donut. Not gussied up with fresh fruit or artisan, local-raw-egg custard, and most certainly not greasy or stale. It was the food I always sought out: well-made and offered at a reasonable price.

Donuts have come so far from traditional that what should be normal has somehow morphed into an ideal. As I thought about this, car after car drove up and people came back out with hefty looking boxes. You will not have to ask them what they bought, there is about a ninety-five percent chance it was donuts. Some may have taken a cinnamon roll or two, it is just that, as I have said, this place specializes.

OX DYNASTY PENNSYLVANIA HICKORY SYRUP

JUNIATA COUNTY
MIFFLINTOWN, PA; (717) 371-7029

Getting out of my car at Ox Dynasty Pennsylvania Hickory Syrup, I did not have to think for a moment about how it got its name—there were at least three huge oxen on hand to greet me. Each one was the size of two or three cows and watched me with the steady confidence of an animal that knew it was king of the farm. This farm is not about oxen though, instead, its owner, Doug Drewes, is deeply committed to bringing back an almost lost sweetener: hickory syrup.

Hickory Syrup is not made from sap like maple or birch; it is made by boiling the sugar out of hickory bark. Doug, who is something of a showman, has the ability to make his syrup in an indoor kitchen, he chooses not to though. Instead, he has three copper cauldrons that sit over open fires in a space watched over by those oxen.

The syrup is first and foremost a testimony to the Native American ability to coax intense flavors from the least obvious of foods. Who thought up the idea of roasting, boiling, and reducing hickory bark? What did their friends say when they tasted it? It must have been a culinary genius moment.

Back to the cauldrons. In each one is a heap of roasted hickory bark covered with water, brought to a simmer, and cooked until the hickory bark sugar is extracted. This resulting liquid is what Doug calls "tea." He decants it and starts cooking again. It soon reduces to a syrup that is then filtered and bottled.

When Doug started making the stuff, he knew he was saving a historic artifact of a recipe and was also a bit amazed to realize that he was getting something delicious from what was otherwise sawmill waste. What he did not know was how ready the market was for it. Wherever he went, he would sell out quickly. Home cooks wanted a natural sweetener, chefs wanted a flavor that complemented hickory wood smoking, local food enthusiasts were looking for things native to Pennsylvania, and health food fans wanted a new sweetener that was completely without synthetic chemicals or additives.

Even though hickory syrup is a Native American tradition that predates the European settlement of Pennsylvania, it is something new too. Only a handful of other producers sell it and they all share

Foods to Look For: Outdoor Farmers' Markets

These days, we all know the sight—a cluster of white tents with hand-painted signs surrounded by a gaggle of parked cars and box trucks. They are farmers' markets and we see them all over the place. Suburban towns have them and big city neighborhoods do too. In rural Pennsylvania, where farms are more likely to be struggling home places than industrial giants, people are going to the local farmers' market, connecting with neighbors, and rebuilding the local food systems that once kept our state afloat.

Actually, Pennsylvania has two different market traditions. The first is indoors, and the other is outside. This entry will explore those that are outdoors. Indoor markets—often called "market houses" are a whole separate story. Do not forget that the Easton Farmers' Market (see p. 62) and the Meadville Market House (see p. 126) are both. Outdoor vendor areas sit just a few steps away from indoor market buildings.

How did a whole new universe of farmers suddenly appear with produce for these markets? The Keystone State is filled with vacant and underused plots of farmland, most too small for industrial-scale growing, but the perfect size to fill a local market stand one day a week. Imagine this all-too-common situation: An unemployed construction worker and his teacher wife live on the four-acre remnant of what was once the family farm. Suddenly, the guy sees those white tents popping up in a nearby town and realizes he can put those four acres to good use. His grandpa made a living from that land, so why not him?

Then you can add the back-to-the-landers. They came out of hippie culture and attempted to grow their own food and create their own economy. Only a small handful managed to pull this off, but a much larger group came away from the experience with a patch of ground and excellent farming skills. When they started to see the white tents pop up, their farming instincts were re-awakened. They could grow the stuff, head into town, sell, schmooze, and re-connect.

Thirty years ago, there were only a couple of outdoor farmers' markets in the state. There was the one in

Fresh asparagus, straight from the farmers' market

Leaves of Swiss Chard from a Berks County farm market

Easton (see p. 62) and maybe a few roadside pop-ups in Amish country. Not anymore—big cities today restore, revive, or even create new markets to show how livable they are.

What really stands out at those outdoor markets is the way they are so intensely seasonal. Vendors (usually) have to grow what they sell and sell what they grow so they can keep their space. That means that one week, everybody will have piles of asparagus, and the next week none; then zucchini and cucumbers.

Soon after, eggplants and peppers will join the party, and then broccoli, cabbage, and cauliflower. It is the same with fruit. First will be berries, followed by peaches, and finally apples, pears, and pumpkins.

Headhouse in Philadelphia (see p. 84) leads the urban pack, and places like State College set the pace for smaller cities. You will find them in snazzy tourist towns like Lititz, and distant

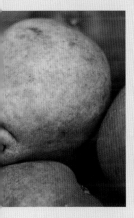

mountain places like Clarion. Are they just for the wealthy? Or maybe just places for farmers to sell a few extra vegetables. In my experience, they are far more than both of those.

Farmers' markets offer one great theoretical advantage over supermarkets and big box stores—you are face-to-face with the producer when you make your purchase. Just as often though, you will buy from a student or part timer who could have been working at those mega-stores except for the luck of the draw.

The foods themselves are your neighbors too. Everything from cucumbers to dry-aged steaks come from nearby. Sometimes there are strict rules about this and they are worth checking. Neighbors know what neighbors are up to. Somebody who is not on the up-and-up will stand out.

And also—and just like the mega-stores—expensive and overpriced items can sit right next to the biggest bargains out there. At one market recently, I found beautiful bell peppers for fifty cents each right next to five-dollar wood-fired soft pretzels. Some people will snap up the deals and leave, others will let those low prices give them permission to buy something expensive. I think it works that way in the supermarket too.

A pot of hickory syrup on the fire at Ox Dynasty in Mifflintown

the same problem; getting enough supply to meet the demand. This has to make you wonder what other specialties are hidden here— what else you cannot find because too many people have forgotten how to make it.

Doug's farm is not open to the public, but he is an outgoing sort and offers his syrups at shows and fairs all over the state. Sometimes, he'll have a table with bottles, pictures, and pamphlets, and on rare occasions, he'll bring his oxen too. You have to see them!

PAPPY'S ORCHARD AND BAKERY

LEHIGH COUNTY
2576 CASSEL RD., COOPERSBURG, PA 18036;
PAPPYSORCHARD.COM; (215) 679-3981

There are lots of farms that offer a few pies or cookies, and a few more that claim to be whole bakeries. In fact, I have been to "farmers' markets" that really should be called "baker's markets." (Although not in Pennsylvania thankfully.) Pappy's is the exact opposite; a bakery that grows its own fruit. You do not come here for a few peaches and pick up a pie, you come here for a pie and maybe a peach or two in addition.

I did not even have to go in. As I was strolling toward the entrance, a guy approached me with a pack of butter cookies and said, "You have to try these!" I took one and agreed. In fact, I was thrilled. Not just because he was twice my size and in command of a huge vehicle, but because he knew his cookies.

Even though it is only a short drive from Allentown and Bethlehem, Pappy's feels remote and actually slow. Sitting at one of the outdoor tables, the thought of staying long enough to watch the fruit ripen does not seem so absurd. On a hot summer day, something baked may be appealing, but a walk through the orchard was even more so. It is not the huge sort of place you see in Adams County, but it is more than just a few trees. Think smaller than a farm and bigger than the biggest of suburban back yards.

There is a kind of orchard air. Inhale it and take in the fragrance of ripening fruit. Enjoy it, and then

An apple tree at Pappy's Orchard

Top: The sign welcoming you to Pappy's Orchard and Bakery
Bottom: Peaches on the tree at Pappy's Orchard

head into the shop/bakery. There are loaves of bread that look like the ones they sell in Pennsylvania Dutch Country, but far less sweet. And then there are those cookies and pies made with the fruit you see growing outside.

The back freezer holds the most interesting things though. Unbaked Cornish pasties, frozen containers of chicken corn soup, and corn pies. Dutch/Cornish fusion food. I got carried away. There are lots of British place names around here and I started speculating about the origins of those pasties. Lisa, the baker, just shrugged. No, there was not an undiscovered subculture of Cornish food here. I was disappointed. Pasty lover that I am, I had dreamed of more.

"Fruit is only seasonal" Lisa told me, "but pies are all year long." It was not an offhand comment. This was the philosophy behind the entire operation. Pappy's customers may say, "We look forward to the few weeks a year when Lisa turns the fruit into pies."

Pappy's has one more specialty: cider. They make cider all though apple season. They sell some fresh—that is, unfermented. And some becomes bottled, alcoholic, and sold under the whimsical Snicklefritz label. Both are worth trying.

You may come to Pappy's for a pie and wind up with some fruit or come for some cider and wind up with a loaf of bread. It is best to show up without a shopping list though. You will always find something to get excited about.

PATTERSON MAPLE FARMS

TIOGA COUNTY
119 PATTERSON RD., WESTFIELD, PA 16950;
PATTERSONMAPLEFARMS.COM; (814) 628-3751

Maple Syrup is not complicated. You start with the sap from a maple tree and then all you do is remove the water. If you remove most of it, you will have a thick syrup, take out all and you have crystals of maple sugar. Most of us associate maple syrup with Vermont. After all, Vermont produces lots more syrup than Pennsylvania does. There is plenty of syrup produced here though with trees tapped everywhere. Most of this is hobbyists making a few quarts of syrup each. Patterson Maple Farms is at the other end of the spectrum—it is the biggest maple syrup operation in the state.

Patterson is a long drive from anywhere, and thanks to my GPS, the last six miles or so of it turned out to be on ice-covered dirt roads through dense forests. I often slowed down to look for trees that had been tapped; they are called "sugar bush" in the trade. (Not to be confused with the shrub from the West Coast or the resort in Vermont.) A farm that produces serious quantities of syrup has to be this remote. If it is not in a vast maple forest, there won't be enough sap to fill all those bottles.

Yes, there was lots of sap. Patterson Maple Farms taps about eighty thousand trees in twenty-six clusters. No, they do not use spigots and wooden buckets. Instead, there is plastic tubing that runs from tree to tree. From those tubes, the sap is collected in large plastic or metal tanks.

This sign announces the entrance to Patterson Maple Farms. It's a welcome sight in one of Pennsylvania's remotest areas.

Even though Patterson Maple Farms started as a dairy, they were tapping trees from the first season Orin and Mable Patterson lived there, more than a hundred years ago. As the years passed and new generations of Pattersons joined the team, their maple specialty became more and more of a

The sugar house at Patterson Maple Farms The white stuff is the steam coming from boiling maple sap

strength. Today, they are up there with the big operations in Vermont and Quebec.

As I chatted with farm veteran Linda Neal, tank after tank of sap was delivered to the sugar house. If this was their daily output, we could fill oceans with it, but the trees only give sap a few weeks a year in early spring. When the nights are below freezing and the days warm up to the forties, they produce. Otherwise, it is the off season.

Like I said, the process is simple. First a reverse osmosis machine takes out about half the water from the sap. Then the resulting liquid is boiled down to the syrup we all know using a contraption that looks like a stainless-steel steam locomotive. Even though it takes forty-three gallons of sap to make a single gallon of syrup, there are thousands of gallons of fresh syrup cooling down in stainless steel barrels. As the hot syrup cools, it forms a vacuum seal that preserves it. About a third of it is sold as bulk in those barrels, the rest is packaged as needed.

If you can, try to come to Patterson when the sap is flowing. The air will be filled with the fragrance of maple and the staff excited to be working at full-bore. If you cannot, their store is open all year round. Maple syrup may only be made in the spring, but there are good recipes for it every month of the year.

PENN STATE BERKEY CREAMERY

CENTRE COUNTY
119 RODNEY A. ERICKSON FOOD SCIENCE BUILDING,
UNIVERSITY PARK, PA 16802; CREAMERY.PSU.EDU; (814) 863-9513

Even if you are a student at Penn State, the campus can seem huge and forbidding. Walking the maze of pathways and checking out the different buildings, you can really feel like you do not belong. Surely, there must be some place where visitors can sit down and relax. And there is: the Penn State Berkey Creamery, a cafe, ice cream parlor, and cheese shop located deep in the thick of the college grounds.

Indeed, you cannot describe it by saying what it is near. Penn State is so big that places that seem a few steps apart wind up taking long hikes to reach. So, wherever you may be, the creamery is a welcome destination and worth the walk or bus ride.

The ice cream here is very good, but what makes the Creamery worth a visit is its very existence. Come on over, have a snack, appreciate the sprawling university campus, and use the restrooms. Visitors get their bearings, students bring their parents, and everybody has something they have to study.

What you will find when you get here is mainly an ice cream shop, with cases of sandwiches, coffee, and cheeses for sale. You could come here for lunch and not even touch the ice cream, but few people do that. Instead, the retail and food sections are almost empty and the ice cream line is often fifteen people deep.

You may think that the vast stainless-steel monstrosity behind the glass windows is a scale model of one of those

My cup of Monkey Business—ice cream flavored with banana, peanut butter, and chocolate Great tasting, but too much for an adult visiting alone

Foods to Look For: Pawpaws

All you have to do is mention the word "pawpaw" in parts of rural Pennsylvania and you will start hearing the song. People from all over the region have sung it for me. Most of those singers had something in common; they had no idea what a pawpaw was. They would belt out the words, "Pickin' up pawpaws, puttin' 'em in your pocket," with ease and confidence, and then sheepishly tell me they did not even know they were a food.

And that is just what pawpaws are: a delicious green, tree fruit that is native to parts of Pennsylvania and the areas south and west of us too. Not so long ago, they were an important part of life around here—so important that songs are sung and places are named after them. People are not so good at finding wild foods anymore and pawpaw trees are rarely cultivated, so for those reasons, they do not show up in markets very often. When they do, buy them first and ask questions later.

The fruit may be all-American, but what about the name? Wikipedia says it is a derivative of the Spanish word *papaya*. This would sort of explain how papayas could be called pawpaws on the other side of the world. However, I think that food historian Michael Twitty has a theory that makes a bit more sense. He suggests that both fruit names originated in the African diaspora. Unlike the Spanish, Africans in the diaspora were cut off from both their oral tradition and culture. Using a word that recalled their past made sense, even if it was not exactly botanically correct.

A name with roots in oral rather than written history would explain the many spellings we have seen too. You will see "pawpaw," "papaw," "paw paw," and even "poppaw." The last being the way pawpaw lovers Lewis and Clark rendered the word. (Their expedition ate an awful lot of them.) Our fruit, officially known as *asimina triloba*, has at least a few slang names too. It has been called "Kansas banana," "Indiana banana," "Ozark banana," and "hillbilly mango." These days, people seem to be sticking with "Paw Paw" and "pawpaw."

Here's the thing, they have a taste that is a sort of cross between mangoes and bananas and really look like tropical fruits. If somebody handed you one and told you it only grew in Indonesia, you would believe them. They are all-American though, locally born and raised. Pawpaws never really went away, but as supermarkets became our main food source, pawpaws were ignored. Because they bruised so easily and spoiled so quickly, the

Freshly picked pawpaws

big stores did not like them. They wanted a fruit that could cross oceans and last for entire seasons. So those prime pawpaw patches became condos and malls and all that was left was the song.

Today, pawpaws make it to market in a couple of different ways. Yes, some people will still pick them in the wild and offer them at roadside stands. The majority for sale are cultivated in orchards though. When you see them at the bigger markets, or perhaps at one of the pawpaw festivals that are popping up, they are most likely from a specialist grower.

When you shop for pawpaws, look for a smooth, unblemished, green skin. Growers will bend over backward to deliver them that way. However, hard-core fans will tell you that they are not fully ripened until they have at least a few black spots on them. In any case, pawpaws bought in the greenest purity will reach that blackened stage before you know it.

There is another reason pawpaws never really became popular: the really big seeds you find inside. They are a bit of a challenge to eat and even harder to cook with. Something is changing on that front though. At least one grower has brought in a fruit pitting and cleaning machine and can extract the pulp easily. This paves the way for pawpaw pulp ice cream, smoothies, and maybe even cream pies.

The best way to keep up on the world of pawpaws is to attend a festival. There, you will find those very snacks along with seedling trees, freshly picked fruit, and the advice of experts. They cannot make you enjoy picking out those seeds, but with a few tastes, you will love them despite their flaws.

chemical refineries on the New Jersey Turnpike, it is not—it is the plant where fresh milk is processed into ice cream, cheese, and cream cheese. It dwarfs the dairies of artisans like Valley Milkhouse (see p. 208) and creates a sort of paradox. Is this place too big to make the sort of quality product that many of us expect? Or is it even big enough to educate the next generation of cheese and ice cream makers?

With this in mind, I ordered a cup of a flavor called Monkey Business. Cups of ice cream were served in only one size and it was too large for a healthy adult. Why are we forced to take such absurdly large portions so often? I carried my cup out to the seating area and saw other people struggling with the same issue. So many were asking, "How much of this should I really be eating?"

My cup of Monkey Business, with its banana ice cream, peanut butter swirls, and bits of chocolate was delicious and creative—a fine snack on a hot summer day. My portion was all wrong though—a kind of forced fattening if I ate it all, and a terrible waste if I did not.

I ate less than half and threw the rest in the trash. I was not sure if I should have been proud of my restraint or ashamed of what was left over.

This is everybody's loss. A bit of ice cream should be a food that anyone could enjoy. Instead, the instinct of all too many of us is to first stuff ourselves until we're too fat and then—after a few scares at the doctor's office—stop eating it altogether. Does Penn State have a school of nutrition? Are they studying obesity? If so, this is where they should start.

POUNDS' TURKEY FARM

WESTMORELAND COUNTY
MELWOOD RD., LEECHBURG, PA 15656;
POUNDSTURKEYFARM.COM; (724) 845-7661

Sometimes a random event will change a person's life. And that event could even affect the way future generations make their way through the world. It happened to the late Harry Pounds when he went to a local fair in Indiana County (Pennsylvania, of course) and won some baby turkeys. He had been trying to get a farm going in an area closer to Pittsburgh and had no idea what crop would make it work. If he had won piglets, Pounds' Turkey Farm would now be famous for its ham and bacon, and had it been a goat, they'd be making cheese. He won turkeys though, and his children, grandchildren, and great grandchildren now devote their lives to turkey farming.

Harry had a lucky break. After all, Americans eat a lot of turkey. At the time he brought his first birds to his new farm, most households ate whole roast turkeys at Thanksgiving and Christmas and considered them to be the most seasonal and celebratory of meats. Turkey consumption has changed in the past half century. We eat less of it at Christmas and much more of it the rest of the time. Thanks to this, Harry and his offspring have managed to make their farm work.

The guy was more than lucky though. He chose the Alle-Kiski Valley for a location. It was a perfect spot for retail farming—an hour by car from Pittsburgh and not all that far from a whole bunch of factory towns. Now, Pond's Turkey Farm draws most of its customers from nearby Westmorland and Armstrong Counties. Even though they are not big-city types, they are people who want their food from a farm they can visit themselves.

Not only did Harry start a turkey farm and raise a family on it, but his children are also running it today—talk to them and you can see their passion for it shining through. Even his great-grandchildren are interested. This is a family operation of the highest order.

The farm is not exactly as it was back in the day. In the beginning, they raised heritage turkeys, and during the fifties and sixties it presented a problem. Because of their darker feathers, their skins looked dirty after they were plucked. They finally gave in and switched to pure-white domestic breeds. To this day, they obsess over this, inspecting every turkey carefully. Several members of the

163

Foods to Look For: Pie, or More Precisely, Shoofly Pie

Pennsylvanians eat a lot of pie. You see it everywhere, and constantly find references to it in memoirs and history books. We modern folks think of pie as a food—and a fattening food at that—so we are going to have to turn that around and ask, "What can pie do for us?"

It is a much deeper question than you may first think.

Like I said, pies are a food, and for many rural Pennsylvanians, they are also a medium of exchange. Pies are something that can be made at home, warmly received as gifts, and reliably sold at roadside stands and outdoor markets. In that last sense, they are innocent counterfeit currency; possibly illegal and easy to circulate. Maybe this is why whoopie pies (see p. 18) are called pies. They too share that easy-to-sell charm. Indeed, an article in the *Atlantic Monthly* published way back in 1869 quoted a Pennsylvania Dutch farmer as saying, "We have great faith in pie." There is no reason to suspect that this attitude has changed.

Let's get the facts first; pie is a composed food consisting of a pastry crust that encloses a filling. Of course, all the classics are present in the Keystone State. You can find an apple pie almost anywhere and a chicken pot pie almost as easily. It is just that when people think of Pennsylvania and pie at the same time, they are often thinking of its most legendary local specialty—shoofly pie. Even if we've eaten it, not many of us know what it is made from. It is time to take a look at those Pennsylvania Dutch pies a bit more closely.

Shoofly pie is the totemic product of the Amish kitchen— think of it as the Pennsylvania Dutch form of Bitcoin. You can bake a few and exchange them with strangers for cash. Even if your pie is vile, it won't matter. Most customers are tourists from far away and have little or no idea what it is supposed to taste like. They will have a slice; enjoy the blast of country sweetness, and lavish praise upon it.

For so many bakeries, markets, and restaurants, "shoofly" is all you need to say. Sadly, for quite a few of them, it is the only local thing they have. And while a burger, fries, and a slice of shoofly may not be an uncommon meal in Lancaster County, it does not even scratch the surface of what Pennsylvania Dutch baking offers.

An Amish cookbook on my shelf lists nine different recipes for shoofly pie. All seem to make the same thing; a blob of different sweeteners that are sitting in a pie crust. Molasses is standard and so is brown sugar. Then there is fat; sometimes shortening and sometimes lard, and maybe an egg to firm it up. Bake it all together and cut yourself a wedge of pure sweetness. Look for two variations: the self-explanatory chocolate shoofly and Montgomery Pie, a shoofly pie with added lemon and a cake that somehow forms a top layer.

The signature food of Pennsylvania Dutch Country—Shoofly Pie

Not liking shoofly pie in Amish country is roughly like not liking spaghetti in Italy. Be prepared to embrace it and name a favorite source. Raisin pie is another local specialty that is worth a try. Sometimes the Amish call it "funeral pie" because it can be baked quickly and does not use any seasonal ingredients. Perfect if you have to whip something up for a sudden funeral. After all, what other pie can you make with stuff that most people typically have around the house?

Savory pies are also out there. American chicken pot pies are common of course, and if you frequent British-style pubs or tea shops, you will find "steak" pies too. In both cases, chefs will often swap a puff pastry crust for the more typical pie shells we're used to in order to add a bit of class.

Then there is one more Pennsylvania Dutch thing—a chicken pot pie that really is not. Pennsylvania Dutch cooks have a stew with chicken, vegetables, and noodles in a flour gravy that is called "pot pie" on menus today. It is not a pie of course; it is the modern pronunciation of *bott boi*, the historic name of the dish. "Chicken and noodles" would be a more accurate description. Old ways die hard around here.

Pounds family check the thoroughness of their competitors' work to this day.

Beverly, the current matriarch, told me that once on vacation in England, she and her turkey-crazed husband encountered a whole roast turkey at a buffet. He examined it closely looking for clean feather removal. It was a matter of professional concern.

Production is pretty straightforward. Day-old baby turkeys (called "poults" in farmer jargon) are brought in from the hatchery in groups. They are fed with grain, and after about sixteen weeks, they are ready for slaughter, cleaning, and packing. It is all done on the farm.

Actually, not only do they raise the turkeys themselves, but they also sell quite a bit of it at their on-farm retail store. The store has more than whole birds and parts though, Pounds' is also an industrious producer of ground turkey, turkey-based sausages, pot pies, smoked turkey breast, turkey bacon, and prepared items like half-turkey breasts on beds of stuffing. That last dish is sold frozen with complete cooking instructions. It is perfect for those times when one or two people want a roast turkey dinner.

Even though Beverly had some good stories—everything from television sports producers looking for "sexy" turkeys to show during a Thanksgiving Day game to the times they had to wait for truckloads of hatchery chicks all night in a McDonald's parking lot. She made it clear that the best part of having a turkey farm was being part of their customers' holidays. Thanksgiving wouldn't be the same without a great turkey, and if you happened to be the one who raised it, so much the better.

READING TERMINAL MARKET

PHILADELPHIA COUNTY
51 N. 12TH ST., PHILADELPHIA, PA 19107;
READINGTERMINALMARKET.ORG; (215) 922-2317

If you do not go to the Reading Terminal Market for a year or two, I can promise that many of your favorite vendors will be gone. No matter how much you loved them, it was not enough in this pressure cooker of food retailing. To sell here, you have to please a huge and fast-moving crowd.

Take Valley Shepard (no relation to Valley Milkhouse, see p. 208), it was a thriving cheese maker and vendor that occupied some prime Terminal Market real estate for at least a few years—until it was gone. I would have thought its artisan, farmhouse cheeses (from nearby New Jersey) would have been a perfect match. Oh well.

Some people brush off the Reading Terminal Market for being "just like a food court." Well, I am sorry, but it is not "just a food court." Not at all. It is the best food court in the state and maybe the solar system too. It is not for a mall or an airport; this is a food court for a city of more than a million people. A center of eating and food culture that has appeared because this is what local people want to eat.

Top: A sign welcomes you to the Reading Terminal Market in Philadelphia
Bottom: Even inside, bright neon lights illuminate the scene

It can take a solid hour to walk the market aisle by aisle and it is worth every moment spent. There is no better barometer of what Pennsylvania is eating than this. Of course, there are the classics. For example, Iovine Brothers and its old school produce occupy a big space, there is nothing fancy here and it is all the better for it.

Then the Down Home Diner, a wonderful sit-down restaurant run by Food Network pioneer Jack McDavid. He was there in the kitchen but I could not bring myself to talk to him. Back in 1996 when he was on the air, I watched and dreamed of being a food writer. There was no way I was going to puncture the bubble of my Food Network memories.

Tommy Dinic's is another classic with steak or pork sandwiches. They are shreds of beef grilled with onions and cheese and were named this by and for people who could never expect to get closer to a "real" steak. These sandwiches are a Philadelphia classic and explored in more depth elsewhere in this book. (see p. 100)

Bakers also make the classics list. Metropolitan Bakery with its French breads, croissants, cookies, and bagels is worth a stop. Beiler's has stands on both sides of an aisle—one side for doughnuts and the other for sticky buns and breads. It is not unusual to see lines more than twenty people long in the doughnut zone and a smaller, but still formidable crowd waiting for the sticky buns too.

Butchers require some careful checking. If you are from the neighborhood, you will find an amazing assortment of beef, pork, and poultry. But if you come from other parts of Pennsylvania, you can get the same or better for lower prices elsewhere.

Most of the vendors are not part of the old guard. Nobody can really predict what you will find on any given day. I have noticed baked ziti, Persian sweets, an ever-changing parade of chocolates, medicinal herbs, linen napkins and tablecloths, Thai curries, fresh juices, exotic mushrooms, specialty corndogs, tostones, jerk pork, house-made ketchup, and honey. Many will come and go. Some will be there for a decade or more and still look like interlopers, and others will defy the odds and become the establishment. In the Reading Terminal Market, survival equals success.

An hour before closing on a Monday evening, the vendors were still going strong. Ten or twelve people were waiting for Beiler's doughnuts and others gathered at hot food stands even as the servers washed down the counters. Except for a handful of deeply religious stall owners like the Amish, it goes on seven days a week—in winter it starts before dawn and ends after dark. Yes, it is the food court of a big, hungry city. Luckily, a big, hungry, and welcoming one.

I found that the Reading Terminal Market was constantly playing with my perceptions. The vastness of it forces you to open your mind. You cannot pine for what is missing. The laws of economics will ensure that whatever has replaced it will offer you something good to eat. Wander and become hypnotized. Soon, you will start thinking that every stand is your favorite, that they all sell exactly what you want. When that happens, it is time to put your wallet away and take a rest.

RODALE GREENHOUSES AT RODALE INSTITUTE

BERKS COUNTY
611 SIEGFRIEDALE RD., KUTZTOWN, PA 19530;
RODALEINSTITUTE.ORG; (610) 683-1400

On a sunny day, a visit to the Rodale Institute is one of the nicest garden walks in Pennsylvania. Although the institute may not be a garden in the sense of an actual botanical garden, it is so well-manicured that even when you are walking through the fields, it is more garden than farm. It all makes sense: the Rodale Institute is a sort of visitor's center for the entire organic farming movement—its grounds were the first organic farm in America.

Started by J.I. Rodale back in the 1930s, this is where organic arrived. Yes, J.I. was the guy who went on a popular talk show to plug the organic life and died during the taping. Although that is pretty much all he's remembered for today, in his time, he was the biggest advocate for health food in the county, publishing books and magazines to make his point.

Before visiting Rodale, it would be a good idea if we came up with a clear definition of what organic farming is. Simple enough; organic farming is contemporary, scientific agriculture that does not use synthetic chemicals. If you farm in a way that re-creates historic methods, it could be considered "organic" because you do not use those chemicals, but it is more properly described as "primitive" or "historic" farming because it came before the science. Organic farming as it is done here is modern, clean, and free of synthetic chemicals. Indeed, the institute holds classes and workshops for farmers and gardeners and this is the focus of what they teach.

Top: Garlic Scapes, one of the earliest seasonal vegetables, at the Rodale Institute
Bottom: Apples fruiting on the tree at the Rodale Institute

If you want proof that pesticides are not used here, open your ears and listen. The soundtrack of birdsong is vivid. The fields are alive in the way J.I. Rodale imagined. With lush green fields, happy animals, and a clear-flowing stream, it is the place you wished all your food came from.

More than anything else, this is a great place to ask questions about organic practices. Everybody you talk to knows their stuff. The team here is young, energetic, and articulate. And if casual conversation is not enough, there are presentations and workshops too. Be aware you are in the middle of nowhere—it may be a long, dark drive home when an event here ends.

Speaking of events, it seems like plenty of them happen here. One of the big barns was ready for a wedding the last time I visited. If you want a ceremony in a setting that is not quite garden and not quite farm either, this is your place.

While the institute has a beautiful shop selling seeds, garden supplies, books, and tee shirts, you will be surprised to see that it is pretty tough to actually buy any of the food produced here. Even though there is a chest freezer in a corner with some farm-raised meat, produce is tough to come by. Actually, anything to eat is tough to come by. There is no restaurant, or even snack bar. It leaves you in a funny position—you are asked to believe in the food the Rodale family grew and ate and the science behind it too. It is the food inspired *Prevention*, *Organic Gardening*, and a host of other publications. And you cannot taste it. It seems that taste would be the key. Would a loaf of bread baked with the rye growing in the field by the visitor's center taste better? Inquiring minds want to know.

That bag of frozen organic broccoli you bought in the supermarket the other day is a direct decedent of what was first grown here, and so was that container of organic milk. This farm is where the first shots of the American organic revolution were fired.

THE RED RABBIT DRIVE IN

PERRY COUNTY
60 BENVENUE RD., DUNCANNON, PA 17020;
REDRABBITDRIVEIN.COM; (717) 834-4696

It was a classic mid-July scorcher; 95°F in the shade. You may think that anybody on the highway who needed some lunch would have chosen a place with air conditioning. Maybe most of them did. Not all though. The Red Rabbit Drive In, which has no inside seating at all, was packed.

There are two ways you can eat at The Red Rabbit; most of the customers choose their own cars, where servers bring you your meal on one of those metal trays that hangs from your window. You can also sit at shaded picnic benches, where you eat from the exact same trays. Takeout is also possible, and it is brought to your car by the aforementioned staff.

People of a certain age will call those servers carhops. Their kids will know carhops too. They represent a time that is often depicted on TV and in movies—right before the really big changes of the sixties. Drive ins! *Happy Days! American Graffiti!* It was the backdrop for the American experience of 1962.

In a way, the menu is classic early sixties fare: fried chicken or fish platters, burgers, and ice cream sundaes. It has adapted over the years though and today, you will find

Top: A whole meal served at my car window
Bottom: The sign in front of The Red Rabbit in Duncannon

Searching for Scrapple

PHILADELPHIA COUNTY
DUTCH EATING PLACE AT THE READING TERMINAL MARKET
51 N 12TH ST, PHILADELPHIA, 19107
READINGTERMINALMARKET.ORG; (215) 922-2317

I figured that the best place to start my search for scrapple—the traditional loaf of buckwheat, cornmeal, broth, and mystery meat—was at a serious Amish restaurant. When most people think Amish, they think *rural*—buggies on narrow country lanes, girls in smocks, and corn stalks aiming at the sky. Not me, I had inside information. I knew that the best Amish breakfast was in downtown Philadelphia: The Dutch Eating Place in the Reading Terminal Market (see p. 167) to be precise. As a reward for waking up two hours before dawn and drowning myself in coffee, I expected an other-worldly meal upon my arrival.

Walking past displays of wrap sandwiches, muffins, and croissants, I saw The Dutch Eating Place. One spot in the corner was available and I grabbed it. Seconds later I was face to face with an Amish girl, pad and pen in hand, waiting for my order. I took a single egg over easy with scrapple and toast.

Scrapple is one of those foods that have a zone. Besides the big city of Philadelphia, you find it in eastern and central Pennsylvania, Delaware, and southern New Jersey. Living in the middle of it, I had eaten it more than a few times. If you are from the area, you will know it is a plastic-wrapped gray block that supermarkets shelve in the meat section. Of course, whenever you see a meat product in gray loaf form, questions come up.

On TV shows that depict scrapple making, you would see the leftovers from pig butchery being boiled in large cauldrons. This makes sense; the head and feet (for example) have large amounts of gelatin that would give richness. Bits of meat missed during the initial butchery would fall off the bones and into the liquid, giving it a bit of depth. However, scrapple's real main ingredient is grain. This means that a vegan scrapple, perhaps made with mushrooms and root vegetables, could be perfectly legitimate. You could make vegan scrapple with kohlrabi and rutabaga and scare off the average American eater without any meat at all.

Slices of scrapple in a cast iron frying pan

Scrapple for dinner at the Town Hall Restaurant in Lancaster County

Rumor had it that scrapple was made with strange pig stuff. I wanted to see lists of ingredients for myself. There was only one problem; those people who'd been trying to scare me off scrapple did not know what they were talking about. Scrapple did not contain much offal at all. The choice was fear or facts and they chose fear.

I wanted the iron-y tang of kidney, the fatty bitterness of liver, and that air of the unknown that a truly fine mystery meat carries with it. I will come clean; I wanted the strangers sitting next to me to lean over and say, "You are really brave to eat that!"

On the wall beside me was a photo of Rachel Ray sitting at this very counter and her rave review right next to it. There is no escaping these Food Network stars. But my plate was put in front of me before I could get through the first paragraph. I needed a chance to study the slice of scrapple, so I ate the egg first. My slice was thinner than I expected and so well done it appeared to be nothing but crisp.

I took a bite and it tasted like a delicious polenta. No mistaking it, this was slightly pork-flavored grain; maybe corn, and perhaps a bit of buckwheat too. There was no mystery meat at all. Not even mystery filler. By the fourth forkful, I knew the whole story and started writing it on a little pad I carried in my jacket pocket. The recipe was obvious. It began with some sort of pork soup, then spices and grain were mixed in and cooked. That would make the mixture solidify. If the broth was a bit fatty, slices of the solid pork and corn mixture would brown easily, and if it was sliced thin enough, cook quickly.

Scrapple is always artisan. In the zone, many butchers make their own and sell it at very low prices. I offer only one cooking tip: slicing it thin and cooking it crisp had the potential to bring out some deep meat and grain flavors.

With a bit of book research, I finally understood the last piece of the puzzle. Why was it that scrapple never really tasted of offal? When I started, I expected the flavor of liver and kidney. I figured that scrapple was some way of tricking you into eating guts. A hundred years ago though, nobody had to hide liver or kidneys, they were prized cuts served in fine restaurants. Back then people trashed baby back ribs—or perhaps they boiled them up for scrapple—while they cheerfully downed big plates of sauteed or roasted organs. That may not be us today, but thankfully, the recipe for scrapple hasn't been updated. Broth, grain, and a few lucky meat bits make it up. Like everything else Pennsylvania Dutch, it is mild enough for a baby.

pizza, barbecue, unsweetened iced tea, and, if you look carefully, gelato. It took some careful study to parse out what was history, what was nostalgia, and what was just plain junk food.

A student of American pop culture could spend hours on this, but we food fans will notice that modern touches are pretty much limited to diet sodas, unsweetened iced tea, and French fries with bits of skin still attached. During the glory days, potatoes were always peeled, iced tea was always sweetened, and the only diet soda most people knew was sold in drug stores and meant for diabetics.

My choice on my last visit was a fried haddock platter. Sitting in my car, eating my fish, and fondly recalling my own childhood drive-in meals—the only part of those summer days I did not hate—I fell for The Red Rabbit and wished they were open more often. Normally I wouldn't eat fried fish cut into perfect rectangular slices, but context can count, and sitting in my car, the smell of deep-fried food wafting by. I was living the fast-food dream.

When it opened back in 1964, The Red Rabbit was a sign of the times. It was miles away from the nearest chain fast-food restaurant and right at a major junction of roads that connected the many small industrial towns along the Susquehanna and Juniata Rivers. The chain convenience stores and restaurants that form its main competition today were not even dreamed of yet.

The "Happy Days" of the fifties and early sixties were fading rapidly as The Red Rabbit began its life. During its first decade of existence, Vietnam, the hippie movement, a string of political assassinations, and a host of other big changes turned the Red Rabbit from new to relic in the blink of an eye.

A half a century of progress may have encouraged the managers to add diet soda, barbecue, and gelato to the menu, but the Red Rabbit has held up nicely. Eating in your car may mean different things to different generations—it could be a semi-private place to be with friends, a way to save a few minutes of your precious time, a place to listen to your own soundtrack, or even a chance to pretend to be in a scene from a nostalgia film—no matter. They offer a really simple and well-prepared menu and a very basic setting. You have to bring your own fantasies though.

RISING CREEK BAKERY

GREENE COUNTY
115 MAIN ST., MOUNT MORRIS, PA 15349;
RISINGCREEKBAKERY.COM; (724) 324-5030

Most people would think a small-town cafe like Rising Creek Bakery wouldn't go beyond the basics. After all, many Pennsylvania towns the size of Mount Morris do not have any bakeries or cafes at all. You can get some solid food at Rising Creek, for example, a bowl of granola or a Reuben sandwich. And if you look, you can also find something that was once a staple of Appalachian diets: salt rising bread.

Salt rising bread came about when bakers could not get either yeast or sourdough. In today's world, that seems a bit strange. After all, sourdough cultures are common enough and commercial yeast is sold in every supermarket. This was not always the case though. Packaged yeast is a modern invention and while sourdough has a long history, keeping it alive and healthy enough to bake with is a tough task.

Nobody seems to know how the bread came to be called "salt rising." There is no more salt used in it than any other loaf and it does not taste salty at all. And do not forget that the pioneers who first made it did not have the education in microbiology that many of us get today. They knew their recipe was different, but it is unlikely that they fully understood the difference between yeast and bacteria and how that influences baking and bread.

Without yeast or sourdough, you would think the result would be matzo, but there is another way to get dough to rise—bacteria like *Clostridium perfringens* will do the job and then be killed off by the heat of the bread oven. This wouldn't be anybody's first choice, but in the hands of Appalachian women, it became delicious.

Like just about everything in coal country life, making salt rising bread is a tough task. Sometimes it does not work at all and whole batches of dough have to be trashed. So as yeast became more popular, salt rising bread faded away. It was once pretty common in its home range—that was back then though—today, Rising Creek Bakery is Pennsylvania's last commercial outpost.

When Jenny Bardwell started the place back in 2010, her goal was to create a bakery that would keep the tradition of salt rising bread alive. In fact, she was already something of a salt rising bread fanatic.

Maybe it was her unique education ... she attended both the Culinary Institute of America and University of Massachusetts. That left her with expertise in baking and plant pathology—a perfect combo for a salt rising bread enthusiast.

It worked. The bread and bakery were almost instantly popular. Soon she was baking it in large quantities and making French toast and sandwiches with it too. Jenny herself has since retired, but the current owners are as passionate about the bread as she is.

Top: A loaf of salt rising bread from Rising Creek Bakery
Bottom: Toast made from salt rising bread, a classic from Appalachia

If you want to know the taste of history, this is something you must try. The bakery is right off I-79 and about a mile north of the West Virginia state line. If you are there at breakfast time, you can have some salt rising toast with tomato gravy, which is another local classic. No, this is not the Italian/American sauce, it is an Appalachian adaptation of it—a cross between flour-based sawmill gravy and an Italian tomato sauce. It is about as traditional a breakfast as you will be able to find. Rising Creek ships hundreds of loaves a week to every corner of the country. If you cannot get to Appalachia, one of its most classic foods can come to you.

ROLLING HILLS RED DEER FARM

COLUMBIA COUNTY
63 PINNACLE DR., CATAWISSA, PA 17820;
REDDEERATROLLINGHILLSFARM.COM; (570) 356-7482

Grazing beef cattle are something you would expect to see on the pastures that cover much of rural Pennsylvania. While they are a good and historic choice, some adventurous farmers are trying other animals entirely. You will see sheep of course, and then more unusual creatures like llamas and, at Rolling Hills Red Deer Farm, red deer.

What exactly are red deer? They are the Scottish cousins of American elk and far bigger than our native white-tailed deer. If you were a watcher of the travel and hunting television shows of a generation or two ago, you will know what I am talking about. They are those huge deer that were stalked by guys in kilts who carried really fancy looking shotguns. They became the most prized of British game meats. It is easy to imagine James Bond ordering "roast fillet of venison" in an old-school London men's club.

Rolling Hills Red Deer Farm began back in 1998 when Lloyd George (NOT the former British Prime Minister) and his wife Dolly were touring western Pennsylvania and saw both herds of wild elk and red deer farms offering venison for sale. They were impressed. Those red deer were a stunning sight and the price tag on their meat was impressive too—especially for a down and out cattle farming couple. And venison was not the only revenue stream. People were paying good money just to get a look (and a few photos) and private hunting reserves wanted some too.

By the time the next spring rolled around, pastures on their farm that were once the home of cattle were now filled with red deer. First there were fourteen, then sixty, and not so long after, hundreds. And that is where they are now; between four and six hundred at any given time.

These days, their business is not so different than what they saw a couple of decades ago. Because they are surrounded by campgrounds and near some old resorts, tours are a big deal. Take the hayride/farm package and pretend you are on a Scottish estate. Despite the distinct lack of kilts, you will still see a scene that is a bit more British than Pennsylvanian. While you are there, stop in the farm shop and buy some venison. Most of what they offer are either fillets or packages of ground meat, after all, many of the shoppers are going to be cooking over a campfire. You can also find sausages and cured meats too, and if that is not enough to impress you, they also have venison dog treats. I imagined these as being for James Bond's dog, but instead, they are for dogs that cannot have beef or pork. Sadly, you cannot get the venison chops that those old Englishmen loved so much, even if you beg.

Red deer venison is about the leanest meat you can find. Really lean meat is often described as "healthy" and while that may be theoretically true, I would reserve judgment until I knew how it was going to be cooked. Some cuts can be grilled, some can be braised without adding much fat, and some will have to have extra fat added to maximize their flavor. Otherwise, you may just wind up with a dish that is too tough to eat. And yet, it does not take much to make this meat truly delicious. A roast braised in red wine, a few sausages on the grill, or even a cheeseburger will deliver some truly intense flavor.

There is more than tours and meat, Rolling Hills has something for hunters too. They offer twenty or thirty guided hunts on their own property and provide red deer stags to other hunting reserves. This is a chance to harvest a red deer without traveling to Scotland or New Zealand. Compared to the rest, this is a tiny sideline, but it gives you some sense of the lure that red deer hold with sportsmen.

In the end, it does not matter if you are as sophisticated as James Bond or just a guy with a grill at a local campsite—the venison from Rolling Hills will suit you just fine. The hayride/farm tour sounds like fun too.

SAE HAN FOOD MARKET & TO DAM GOL KOREAN RESTAURANT

MONTGOMERY COUNTY
1341 & 1349 E. TOWNSHIP LINE RD., BLUE BELL, PA 19422;
(610) 272-9554; (BOTH USE THE SAME PARKING LOT)

ASSI PLAZA

MONTGOMERY COUNTY
1222 WELSH RD., NORTH WALES, PA 19454;
ASSIPLAZA.NET; (215) 631-9400

My wife and I had just finished some shopping at a big chain furniture store deep in the Philadelphia suburbs and after a bit too much driving; we had no idea where we were.

We pulled over for a moment and to our complete surprise, there in front of us was a beautiful Korean restaurant and a well-stocked Korean grocery. The fragrances of garlic, chilies, and fermentation that make up Korean flavor assaulted our senses as soon as we got out of the car.

We ate a great dinner and bought two terrific jars of kimchee and could not even guess where we were. It was a Korean cuisine Brigadoon and we often lamented forgetting to record its address. If stumbling on the place once was shock enough, I inadvertently drove past it again a few years later while my GPS was guiding me to a nearby hiking trail. That second time, I took notes, I was not going to miss a place like this again.

Neither the Sae Han Food Market nor the neighboring To Dam Gol Korean Restaurant were all that remote. Indeed, with a GPS showing the way, they turned out to be only a few miles from exit 333 off the Pennsylvania Turnpike. And as I drove up, my heart was racing as I looked forward to my shot at the most strongly flavored cuisine on the planet.

Sae Han may have been a secret for me, but not for the locals; it has been there for over twenty years. Here in this store are the vegetables, fish, meat, and most of all, spices that you will need to make Korean food. Unlike so many specialty grocery shops, Sae Han has little in the way of prepared foods; instead, with its selections of seaweeds, beans,

A stone pot bowl with a fiery chili sauce from the To Dam Gol Korean Restaurant in Blue Bell

grains, noodles, and tofu, it is a place for Korean home cooks.

If that is not your speed, you can grab some frozen dumplings or jars of locally made kimchee. Or you can walk to the To Dam Gol Restaurant a few doors down. Let them show you to a table, take a look at the Korean TV news, and enjoy a pitcher of barley tea while you study the menu.

Korean restaurants usually begin their meals with tiny dishes of pickles and salads called banchan. These tell the whole story. If they are good, the meal will be too. If they are only a few, do not expect much in the way of portions either. At the best—and To Dam Gol is among the best—you will get a serious introduction to the range of flavors and textures that make up the cuisine.

On my most recent visit, eight *banchan* were put in front of me. There was kimchee of course, and marinated root vegetables, bean sprouts, broccoli, and fish cakes too. Here in those eight little dishes was the antidote to the bland stodge that travelers in Pennsylvania are all too often subjected to.

I had a stone bowl of rice and squid in a spicy Korean sauce. Okay, I know, that is really redundant. Korean and spicy go hand in hand. My stone bowl and all-you-can-eat *banchan* left me feeling almost drugged. The kaleidoscope of intense flavors grabbed me and wouldn't let go. My mind and body were vibrating. It was not LSD, but almost. This is food that kidnaps you, food that forces you to see just how powerful a simple meal can be. Except that when you start reviewing the recipes, you will see that it is not simple at all.

Where there is smoke, there is fire. Even though this little strip mall seems like it is out there by itself, just six or seven miles north, you will find the suburban Philadelphia outpost of the Assi Plaza chain. Assi Plaza describes itself in English as "International Food." During my explorations in Pennsylvania, I have found stores that used "International" to mean everything from Peruvian to Croatian. Most often though, it means, "We sell food from a country we do not think you have ever heard of."

While the store seems to be at least three quarters Korean, there is enough other stuff to (barely) merit the "International" label. You will find goods from all over Asia, of course, more kinds of soy sauce than you ever thought possible, those tuna-sized cans of Thai curry paste that I used to cook with decades ago, meat with bones, chickens with heads, and fish with both heads and bones.

"International" goes deeper here. The Mexican section is large and it is only fitting that you can find so many kinds of dried chilies. And there was a whole aisle devoted to Indian too. Could it be an international and global selection of very spicy foods?

If you are craving Korean and can drive deep into the suburbs, these places are worth a visit. They are not far from highways, they pack the requisite Korean flavor punch, and they have their own free parking. With all that garlic and heat, some people call Korean food a dangerous drug. If you agree and you are ready for more, this is where you can get your fix.

Servings of banchan appetizers from the To Dam Gol Korean Restaurant in Blue Bell

SAINT PETER'S BAKERY

CHESTER COUNTY
3441 SAINT PETERS RD., SAINT PETERS, PA 19470;
SAINTPETERSBAKERY.COM; (610) 469-7501

East of Lancaster County and west of Philadelphia's suburbs, you will find an area known as The Hopewell Big Woods. They are wooded hills that separate the nearby fertile valleys of Lancaster County from the suburbs of Philadelphia. This is where you will find Saint Peter's Village, a tiny, abandoned quarry town that has been re-purposed as a tourist destination. It is not a bad place; the buildings are charming, and you will find the stores you would expect with antiques, gifts, and beauty products. I skipped all of them. I was there for the French bakery.

Saint Peter's Bakery is right in town, quiet and intentionally slow. You do not come here to grab a quick lunch. It aspires to be a notch above what you will find in the surrounding towns and pulls it off easily. Sit down in the dining room and get yourself a croissant that actually tastes like the real thing. You can also find very French cakes and pies; a smattering of Italian products, including a few flavors of biscotti; and a nod to the Pennsylvania Dutch culture that surrounds the place in the form of snickerdoodle cookies.

I had a sandwich the first time I visited, but I really came for the bread. There were baguettes, but in Pennsylvania, any loaf that is tubular and too long for a single sandwich is called a "baguette." (If it is short enough for a sandwich, it is "Italian.") Saint Peter's Bakery takes this a step further. Their breads have the sandy finish and unbleached white interior of the best long loaves you will find in France. They have the flavor too; notes of yeast, good flour, and a whiff of the oven they were baked in.

The multigrain loaf had character too. Less sweet than its local competitors, it gave off that healthy aura of grain that is loved by so many of us. The Saint Peter's bakers offered to slice it for me, but that seemed wrong. I took it home whole and showed it off. Once we were eating it, it was obviously not mass-produced. The grain flavor stood out and reminded us this is more than the stuff that supports a sandwich.

If you are in the region, Saint Peter's is a pleasant destination. It has a nice little shopping strip and French Creek Falls, the cascade behind the town, is a great spot for nature lovers and photographers. And the bakery? Its locally roasted coffee, interesting sandwich combinations, and baked goods that may impress a homesick Frenchman make it the centerpiece of the place.

Top: A very rustic-looking sandwich platter at Saint Peter's Bakery
Bottom: A very rustic-looking loaf of bread from Saint Peter's Bakery

SHANE'S CONFECTIONERY

PHILADELPHIA COUNTY
110 MARKET ST., PHILADELPHIA, PA 19106;
SHANECANDIES.COM; (215) 922-1048

When I stepped through the door at Shane's Confectionery, right in the heart of Philadelphia's Old City, I spotted a tray of fruit slices. Not pieces of fresh fruit of the sort you may see in a salad bar, but rather, those brightly colored jellied sugar candies that sort of look like fruit if you did not eat real fruit too often.

It is not really that sort of candy store. Shane's is vintage in a sense—they work hard to maintain the twenties décor that has been there since . . . well . . . the twenties. And yes, they sell Turkish Taffy, it is just that that is not the main thing. While the vintage touches are a pleasure to see, it is the modern Shane's that makes the place worth a visit. Go for the vegan Thai flavor truffles, artisan chocolate bars, and single-origin drinking chocolates and enjoy the décor while you are there.

In the context of the twenty-first century passion for craft, the superb vintage décor has a way of making the place seem even more contemporary. It does not matter if you are in front buying candy or in the back with a cup of drinking chocolate, this is a modern, serious take on what chocolate can be.

That back-room cafe has only a handful of choices and even fewer places to sit. Two tables and four chairs in a narrow corridor are it. Six kinds of drinking chocolate, brewed chocolate, and an optional house-made marshmallow are the menu. Dedicated fans will rule out the novelties like peppermint or chili and go straight for the single origin. You have the choice of four- or eight-ounce cups. The four is plenty for anybody and the optional marshmallow adds even more richness.

Order a drinking chocolate, sit down at one of those tiny tables, and start sipping. It combines lusciousness and intensity in a way that only chocolate can. As you have more of it, new layers of flavor appear along with the realization that so much of what passes for chocolate is little more than fat and sugar. This is the real thing and you will taste true flavor. Shane's also offers "brewed" chocolate for people who think the drinking chocolate is too much. Of course, I never tried it. I am an all-or-nothing sort of chocolate fan.

A mug of hot chocolate with a house-made marshmallow at Shane's Confectionery in Philadelphia

There are times when I suggest you do not go—when you want to avoid finding yourself too deeply involved with another food or another flavor—I do not want Shane's back room to be the place where I pushed you over the food fixation cliff. Yet, if you have been fascinated by single-origin chocolate, Shane's can be the portal to a wormhole of obsession. Fans of single-origin coffees and single-malt whiskeys will discover a whole new food group.

Shane's also sells packed boxes of their candies and I imagine some people would think that one of them would be a perfect Valentine's Day gift. I must disagree though; a true romantic would know that a cup of drinking chocolate at one of those tiny back room tables is the ultimate experience. Nothing in a box could possibly compare.

SHENANDOAH'S POLISH AND PENNSYLVANIA SAUSAGE CULTURE

SCHUYLKILL COUNTY

CAPITOL FOOD MARKET, 102 E. WASHINGTON ST., SHENANDOAH, PA 17976; (570) 462-0265

KOWALONEK'S KIELBASY SHOP, 332 S. MAIN ST., SHENANDOAH, PA 17976; KIELBASY.NET; (570) 462-1263

LUCKY'S CORNER DELI, 720 W. CENTRE ST., SHENANDOAH, PA 17976; (570) 462-1447

When you explore Pennsylvania's foodways, you eat a lot of sausage. They are a sort of state-wide cultural glue. Maybe they are Polish, maybe they are German, and maybe they are Italian, but they are sausage. As I drove up I-81 toward the old coal town of Shenandoah, I pondered the possibilities. Three of the best Polish sausage makers in the state were there and I was ready.

Soon I turned down a street of old industrial buildings and found Capitol Food Market tucked in among them. Outside, it looked like a farm country feed store that was somehow wedged into a strip of car repair shops. There was a porch with an awning over the main door, and there in the shade was a white board listing five different kinds of "*kielbossi*," two kinds of *krakowska, babka, kishke*, pierogies, and even meatballs.

Inside, it was almost empty. There was a woman talking to the guys behind the counter, and a whole bunch of bare shelves. The coolers were another story entirely. Inside one was a small and spectacular looking selection of smoked sausages. They were the color of polished walnut and giving off the sort of fragrance that old folks associate with childhood campfires. These were called "*kielbossi,*" and when I questioned the spelling, the answer was a shrug.

I mean . . . this place did not really sell anything else. In fact, the menu board outside also listed something called "*krakowska*," but I was so enraptured with the *kielbossi* that I did not notice it. It did not matter. If you could make sausages like those, why would you even bother with anything else?

Kowalonek's Kielbasy Shop at the other end of town was a whole lot more like what many would recognize as a Polish deli. Besides, those sausages—spelled "*kielbasy*" here—there were other house-made cold cuts, and freezers filled with soups and pierogies too. Of course, I asked about the spelling. The woman serving me suddenly got serious. "This is the way my great-grandfather spelled it when he wrote down the recipe back in 1911."

Her tone was impossible to challenge. What if the great-grandfather of the owners of Capitol spelled it differently back then too? It may well have been that neither had enough Polish education to spell this word correctly—even if they spoke the language fluently. (Imagine how your English spelling would be if you never had a lesson.) Or maybe these spellings reflected regional differences that have been lost in immigrant history.

Was there a point to all this? Yes. If they were using modern Polish spellings, it meant they had some contact with modern Polish food culture, that they were part of the bigger (and rapidly growing) world of Polish cuisine. This was different. Nobody spoke the language. Nobody offered anything that their butcher-ancestors did not make.

At Kowalonek's, I bought a container of hot bologna (see p. 12), a Pennsylvania classic, and some of that *krakowska*—a lean pork sausage—too. The sample slice held so much deliciousness that it lingered in my mind and body until long after I drove away. It was not just smoke, there was pig meat that you could bite into and a subtle hint of spice too.

Top: Hot bologna
Middle: Kielbasa slices
Bottom: Note the unusual nickname for Sopressata.

This beat old coal mining town harbored some extraordinary food artisanship. I struggled for a nickname. *"Kielbassa* Island?" *Kielbassa* Mountain?" Whatever, it was the perfect place for a sausage maker to practice their craft undisturbed.

The place is legendary for its Polish sausage and is home to Mrs. T's pierogi factory too, and yet, besides those butchers, there was no sign of Polish food at all. No restaurants, no cafes, no real Polish section in the supermarket. It was a cold winter day and the sorts of foods you would think a town proud of its Eastern European heritage would be happy to serve up were not there at all. My lunch should have been hunter's stew or pierogies and I wound up with empanadas instead. There was not anything wrong with them except for the fact that they clashed with the food in my brain.

Lucky's Corner Deli tricked me in another way—it was not on a corner. It was a cinder block building next to a Family Dollar store. The parking lot offered the sight of smoke pouring out of a kitchen chimney. The art of meat curing seemed to be alive here too. Inside, there were tables and chairs, so I asked a woman behind the counter if they had any Polish food. By this point, I was desperate.

She told me they had a "Polish torpedo" sandwich. While this seemed clever, it did not strike me as being Polish enough. Before I could work myself up to a rant, a glass vat of cured sausages soaking in oil caught my eye. Italians would call them Soppressate. A century of American coal miners morphed that word to "soupys." Of course, I bought one. I had to.

Driving west from Lucky's, I passed by miles of strip mines, their heaps of coal sitting and waiting for just one more steam locomotive. Like those Shenandoah sausages, they were remnants of former greatness. While the butchers I visited used Polish names for some of their products, what I bought was mostly Pennsylvanian. They were trying to hang on to their family legacies, but they wound up with a whole new product.

Sausages have power.

Important note: Many of the kielbasa products you will find in Pennsylvania artisan butcher shops look like they can be eaten raw, but are meant to be cooked. Always ask!

SOUL HOUSE CAFE

DAUPHIN COUNTY
1852 NORTH ST., HARRISBURG, PA 17103;
SOULHOUSECAFE.YOLASITE.COM; (717) 236-3500

As you explore the nooks and crannies of Pennsylvania, you will discover food from every corner of the world. Between sausages, stir fries, and curries, you would think we have the whole planet covered, and yet, there is one country that never seems to get the attention it deserves—the United States. Even the indigenous foods of our own state are tough to locate and foods from a few states away are harder to find than the most esoteric dishes from the world's far corners.

That is where the *S*oul House Cafe comes in. There is not much to it; a takeout window and a few picnic tables on a residential street, but the food it offers is the cuisine of the African American South. A genre that is talked about far more often than it is cooked.

Its modest chalkboard menu is authentic and tasty. I had fried chicken. I could not decide if my choice was iconic or corny until it was put in front of me. It turned out to be neither; instead, I was served two pieces of perfectly fried boneless chicken breast. I stared, took a bite, and stared some more. It was greaseless, juicy, and deeply

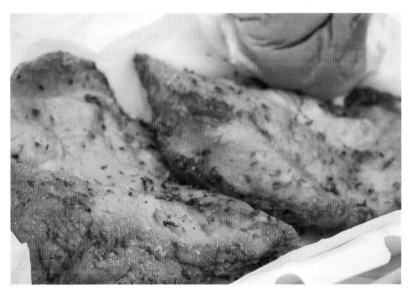

Fried boneless chicken breast from the Soul House Cafe

seasoned without being too hot. This is what those chicken sandwich places were trying to do—only most of them were not doing it half as well.

I had a couple of sides, potato salad and something that was just called "greens." I was served a cup of long-cooked, chopped up green vegetables. A growing lunch crowd prevented me from asking about the details though. For me, that intense cup of greens left the best at the bottom—the cooking liquid. After I finished eating, I slugged it down like a shot of whiskey. A bit of fluid vegetable life. There is more on the menu. I saw cabbage, yellow rice, dirty rice, and two sweet potato desserts—a pie and a cheesecake, I will have to return another time, I was so full I could not manage more.

Soul House Cafe is not located in the most beautiful of neighborhoods, Harrisburg has seen some tough times and you may notice a few scars. This is absolutely not the sort of place that wealthy suburbanites would come to for a leisurely afternoon of shopping. What it is though is one of the friendliest blocks I have ever eaten in. Sit at one of the porch tables and people strolling by will ask you what you ordered and how you like it. The team here is proud of what they have done and what they cook. After all, a thriving and successful kitchen in a neighborhood like this one is a formidable accomplishment.

Sadly, there is no dining room here, so you will have to make sure your southern food cravings hit on fair weather days. Maybe you will eat at one of those (very few) tables outside on the porch, or maybe you will head over to Reservoir Park and the National Civil War Museum. It will certainly be worth your while.

STANDING STONE COFFEE COMPANY

HUNTINGDON COUNTY
1229 MIFFLIN ST., HUNTINGDON, PA 16652;
STANDINGSTONECOFFEECOMPANY.COM; (814) 643-4545

Real coffee fanatics may well enjoy the smell of roasting when they enter Standing Stone Coffee Company in the college town of Huntingdon, but it is not the smell that gets you, it is the sound—the distinctive noise of raw coffee beans tumbling in the roaster. This is coffee culture at its real-est. You order your coffee, and just a few feet away there is a roasting machine running full-bore. Standing Stone does not have a roasting facility, it is a roasting facility.

If you are the sort of person for whom live coffee roasting is a form of entertainment, Standing Stone offers a show—they often roast more than a hundred pounds of coffee beans a day. Questions are always answered and watchers are always welcomed.

In my own travels through deepest, rural Pennsylvania, Standing Stone has become something of a beacon. A place to rest, to write, and to enjoy some coffee in what may other-

The sign out front at Standing Stone Coffee

wise be called the "middle of nowhere." It is near State College, near the Big Valley, and not that far from a whole bunch of other places listed in this book. Wherever I may be, I always think of stopping at Standing Stone for a break before I head back east.

Standing Stone is in a neighborhood of modest homes a few blocks from Juniata College—one of Pennsylvania's most remote campuses. It may be a long way from anywhere, but it is really welcome where it is. Come in and sit down with the locals: students, retirees, Mennonites, and maybe even a professor or two.

Online reviewers always seem to be complaining about how slow things are at Standing Stone. You may be better off if you thought about how slow central Pennsylvania is in general. It is really tough to imagine a person in a big hurry winding up in Huntingdon. It is not a bustling place, just one where people go to college and do more than a small bit of serious thinking.

The team knows you are unlikely to be in a hurry. They themselves are not in much of a hurry either. Instead, they are focused on doing things right—properly roasted high-quality coffee beans and correctly brewed coffee drinks. They know you are here for a while and if they goof up, they know you will still be around to remind them.

Go on in and place your order. It is more than pleasant. Join the local crowd for excellent house-roasted coffees, something to eat alongside them, and in the back, a connected laundromat. On a hot day, you can get iced coffee served in a real glass and the rest of the year, something warm to soothe you. This is the sort of serious coffee that opens your mind.

The location is long and narrow. The front is the cafe itself, just behind it is the roasting area, and in the back are the the washers, and dryers. On one hand, this really surprised me; on the other, I believe that every coffee shop needs a laundry—something practical to do while you are drinking coffee with your nose buried in the screen of some electronic device.

Love of coffee counts here, but it is more than that. It goes back to the days when coffee was always a catalyst for thought, for bonding, and for relaxation. Hurrying here misses the point. You may as well stay; you are not going to get anywhere else all that quickly anyway.

STATE COLLEGE: CHINATOWN 2.0

CENTRE COUNTY

BIG BOWL NOODLE HOUSE
418 E. COLLEGE AVE., STATE COLLEGE, PA 16801; BIG-BOWL-NOODLE-HOUSE.BUSINESS.SITE; (814) 308-9026

LITTLE FOOD COURT
250 E. CALDER WAY, STATE COLLEGE, PA 16801; (814) 826-2189

TOMMY'S ASIAN GRILL
432 E. COLLEGE AVE., STATE COLLEGE, PA 16801; (814) 954-8116

The plate of *mapo dofu* I was facing held me in the gastronomic equivalent of a full nelson. When I could muster enough strength to look up, it was easy to see I was in a room filled with people enjoying their Sichuan food as much as I was. My Corvette-orange heap of bean curd was a dish on the cusp. Common enough to be recognizable by American diners and Chinese enough to count as comfort food for people who were really far from home.

At The Little Food Court, a few blocks from the Penn State campus, I was the only customer who did not fall into the second group. There were at least twenty or twenty-five other diners and it was reasonable to guess most of them were Chinese.

In Philadelphia, you would call such a scene "Chinatown," and here in State College, I would do the same. These days, the Asian food scene in State College is developing so rapidly you can smell soy sauce in the air.

On one hand, it is a town with more than a hundred

A bowl of shredded pork noodle soup from Tommy's Asian Grill in State College

thousand residents. It has an airport, a couple of big highways, and even bus service from New York. On the other, if you are in any other town of a hundred thousand, State College is really far away. It takes a half a day to drive there from Philadelphia and even longer from Washington, DC. State College is big to start with and when you add in the student population, you have the third largest city in Pennsylvania, easily dwarfing Harrisburg, Allentown, or Scranton.

A side dish of green vegetables at the Big Bowl Noodle Shop in State College

Comparing the Chinese food in State College with that of China seemed a bit excessive but seeing how it stacked up to Chinatowns in Philadelphia, DC, and New York was reasonable enough. After my meal at the Little Food Court, I decided to search for iconic Chinatown dishes and give them a try.

Whenever I am in a Chinatown, I see the same dynamic; everybody loves menus with off-putting items like pork kidney or blood cakes and almost nobody ever orders them. And then, after chuckling at the stuff we do not care to try, we all go for those bowls of rice or noodle soup or big plates of stir-fry. A despondent and homesick Chinese student may go for exactly what the rest of us fear, so we have to be both ready and accommodating.

A little place called Tommy's Asian Grill on one sign and Xi'an Grill on another drew me in. Bright green walls gave it a pop of energy, almost complete silence made it a perfect place to study, and only a few dishes from the long menu were in English.

I ordered "Hand ripped noodles with beef." It turned out to be a really delicious head-scratcher. My noodles were tossed with spicy oil and vinegar and topped with bits of cooked Napa cabbage and thin slices of beef—Chinese soul food. Nothing fancy here, but there was an unexpected echo of kimchee flavor in the bowl. It was classic Xi'an—a cuisine really popular in New York right now.

The other customers spoke Chinese with an easy confidence and sat with their noodles and books as if this were their normal. It was a resounding reminder that universities are global villages. Even though State College was in the middle of nowhere, people come from the far corners of the world. It was truly Chinatown 2.0.

Are the most comforting China-town dishes served in big bowls? Probably. And with that, I went downstairs to a place called Big Bowl Noodle House. Ten minutes before it was opening, there was already a line forming. Snow was falling in flakes the size of marbles and a big bowl of noodle soup seemed awfully appealing. The growing crowd may not have all been Chinese, but most of them could speak the language.

The door finally opened and we all spilled in. It still took a few more minutes to place my order—fish with pickled mustard greens and rice noodles in soup and a side of green vegetables. I

This is the sign for The Little Food Court in State College, an outpost of Sichuan cuisine

was the eighteenth person to order and that gave me a chance to see what the seventeen people in front of me had chosen. Almost nobody got their food in a bowl.

Most of it was stir-fried. Heaps of noodles, heaps of vegetables, and heaps of meat too. It did not go too quickly. I had more than twenty minutes to study orders before mine came out. Indeed, by the time I picked up my own, there were almost no seats left.

I was so distracted by the crowds that I almost forgot about my food. It was a bowl of textures. Fish that was flaky and a tiny bit soft and crunchy pickled cabbage, all in a broth with a distinct vinegar tinge. Then there was my side of greens; what everybody in China orders to make sure they get their daily dose of vegetables. I was proud to have finished both.

It was finals week and people were really shoveling it down. Food for energy, food to relieve stress, and food to remind yourself that you are still human after all that cramming. It was too big a crowd for me to think of it as a small club. I ate along with the best of them though. When my food was finished, I stepped back out and into the falling snow. I was ready for anything.

SUNBURY MARKET HOUSE

NORTHUMBERLAND COUNTY
436 MARKET ST., SUNBURY, PA 17801;
SUNBURYMARKETHOUSE.COM; (570) 286-5801

It is all too easy to think that market houses are just for tourists. After all, they are the first place you are supposed to visit when you go to London, Seattle, or even Philadelphia (see the Reading Terminal Market on see p. 167). Then there is Sunbury. The Sunbury Market House is most certainly not for tourists—nothing in Sunbury is for tourists. It is one of those few remote market houses that still serves its original purpose of providing fresh, local food for the town.

Walk on in. It is lit with florescent tubes, has a white tile ceiling like a dentist's office, and a cement warehouse floor. People are excited to come here—indeed, they are excited the place exists at all. There is a good mix of fresh local and commercial produce, two or three stands with good solid home cooking, a butcher, a deli, and a baker. All both cheaper and higher in quality than the local supermarket. There is also a vendor with a few groceries, and somebody selling stuffed animals too.

I started with the cooked food. I had to. Who could resist pierogies that look like empanadas and empanadas that look like pierogies? And then I reminded myself that they are all dumplings. The empanadas, filled with beef or chicken and served with a mild dipping sauce were fun, but not quite a meal. The pierogies came on a plastic plate with bits of Polish sausage and fried onions. They were hearty enough to hold a person all day.

Tables sit right next to the cooked food stands and offer a full immersion in Sunbury life. Sit down, start listening, and gently offer your opinion when you are asked. By the time I finished my pierogies, I knew more about Sunbury than I felt I had the right to.

Heading over to the butcher seemed like it would be easy yet I was delayed by at least one model train just like one owned more than half a century ago. Even meat could not pull me away from the siren song of nostalgia. When I finished wallowing in my misspent youth, I began to notice how, in Pennsylvania, every butcher is also a smokehouse. There were roasts, pork chops, and even a nice heap of kielbasa.

Produce was represented by two vendors. These were not nearby farms; instead, they sold a mix of wholesale and local items that ensured the best prices. This seemed to work, everything was at least a third less than in supermarkets or more urban farm stands. Was it as perfect? Maybe not, but it was a great value for your money.

Unlike many market houses, Sunbury allows its vendors to cook at their stands. And with that, there is lots of takeout food. Some is made right in front of you and more is frozen. This seems like a good compromise—it is already cooked by somebody you know and just about ready to be eaten. There is an odd twist to this though. The market may allow cooking, but

The entrance to the Sunbury Market House

it does not have gas hookups for commercial stoves. This means that all this food is cooked on rows of household electric stoves—bigger pots and more food than you've ever seen on a home range. It is quite a sight.

I have never spent the night in Sunbury, but if I did, I would certainly check out the dance hall in the back of the market. The two are attached and use the same restrooms but there is never a time when they are both open. That is not all there is. Look for the cafe, hot dog shop, and ice cream parlor on the same block. Sunbury is a long way from anywhere and every one of them is a welcome stop.

TALKING BREADS

CUMBERLAND COUNTY
1619 W. LISBURN RD., MECHANICSBURG, PA 17055;
(223) 800-8394

Great bread is never just there for you. The best bakers rarely put themselves on display, you have to be a seeker. That is certainly the case with Talking Breads. It is not Pennsylvania's most remote bakery (for that you will have to check out Wildfire Breads, see p. 214), but it is a rural destination and not really on the way to anywhere.

Why you have to go that far out of your way for a good loaf of bread is one of the great mysteries of Pennsylvania food culture. After all, to make it, you just mix flour, leavening, and water. A bit of salt could go in too. Get it right, pop it in an oven, and you have bread. It is just the sort of thing that compels a few serious artisans to aspire to greatness. In Pennsylvania we find poor quality bread everywhere; too soft, too sweet, and offering no hint of the wonderful flavors present in those original ingredients.

And that is the real problem. Bad bread can be made and sold cheaply, and bread that looks right but is nothing more than a blob of dough conditioners, food coloring, and sugar can be even more profitable. Good bread, that magic mixture of nothing more than flour, yeast, and water requires great skill and passion to create.

Talking Breads is one woman's attempt at creating a farmstead bakery. Actually, this is not even her first attempt. I first encountered Shana and her bakery at a previous and even more remote location in Perry County. Even there, she drew crowds. The number of people who seek great bread is small, but dedicated. And let's face it, a nice afternoon drive to rural, central Pennsylvania is not a bad way to get a few loaves.

Things did not work out in Perry County though. An ambitious, on-farm, artisan bake shop was not something neighbors were interested in. Shana tried a few different places and finally settled on a location near the town of Mechanicsburg. It is a spot that is rural, and not that far from Harrisburg, the state capitol. A farm shop there would be welcome.

I dropped in the first day they were baking bread. I pulled into their lot while Shana and a helper were kneading and portioning a huge quantity of dough. The bread may not have been ready, but the coffee pot was on and the display case held cookies and pastries—or so I thought. During the time it took me to take a few pictures, most of the case was picked clean.

She'd made cookies from rye and chocolate. Now, these are two classic flavors, just not together. In my mind, the combination seemed strange and I figured if they could get that bit of craziness to taste good, they could do anything. Somehow, it worked. The two deep base flavors of rye and chocolate supported each other and made the cookie one of the most interesting things I had ever eaten in a Pennsylvania bakery.

And then came an everything bagel. Despite its overwhelming everything-ness with seeds of every sort forming a blanket, its bread flavor came through. Tender and not too huge, it was a rare rural bagel of quality. Olive bread was good for the genre, but remained something of a novelty for me. I mean . . . bread can be great and olives can be great, but there is no reason to make one taste of the other.

Finally, there was the whole wheat, sourdough *miche*—a dome of bread that exploded with actual bread flavor. No need to add olives or seeds or dried fruit. It was the flavor so many bakers had forgotten. The oven was not wood-fired, but there was still a bit of char at the bottom of the loaves. This was real food—eat it and you can imagine how it was such an important staple.

Talking Breads wants to be more than just bread; they are putting in cafe tables, a cooler for local cured meat and dairy products, and a coffee bar too. It is the bread that will keep you coming though. There is plenty of good coffee around, and decent pastries to go with it, but that bread . . .

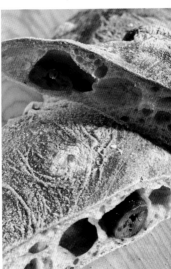

*Top: Welcome to Talking Breads
Bottom: A loaf of olive bread from Talking Breads (note the actual olives)*

THE TEAPARKER TEA HOUSE

CENTRE COUNTY
34 RITENOUR BLDG., UNIVERSITY PARK, PA 16802; NO PHONE

Located deep in the middle of the Penn State campus, it took me a few tries to find The Teaparker Tea House. Even when I was in the right building, students with classes just a few doors away did not know of its existence. At one point, I became so frustrated that I started pointing out tea shop signs to passers-by. Things got better as I went deeper into the building's basement. First, I found a room fitted out for a Japanese tea ceremony. And after that, The Teaparker itself.

The door was open and there was one guy there checking his phone. He asked me to remove my shoes and then told me the place was closed for exam week. Couldn't he have told me that with my shoes on? I asked him a string of questions and he answered each with a succinct, "No." No, there was not any way to find out if The Teaparker was going to be open or closed. No, he could not offer any more details. No. No. No.

A few weeks later, a note popped up on my phone—The Teaparker would be open the following Wednesday. Construction had made the place even harder to find, but I stuck with it and was soon standing at the door. Properly prepared this time, I removed my shoes without prompting and entered.

Do you know those stories where the hero tries his best to gain entry to a heavily guarded secret kingdom, and when he finally gets in, he finds himself warmly welcomed? I was living it. Suddenly, tiny cups of tea were being thrust in front of me, even before I sat down.

It was a cramped basement room filled with college students enthusiastically brewing and drinking tea. I imagined a sort of cafe/tearoom, but this was more of a showroom—a place where the best Asian teas could be properly brewed and sampled—combined with a clubhouse.

One thing you cannot do at The Teaparker is have a pot of tea for yourself. Everything ordered is for everybody present. This explains how at least two cups of it were offered to me before I even took my coat off.

You will find a menu of the teas available. The details can change, but there are basic groups; green, white, red, oolong, and Pu'er. Most of us have drank enough green and oolong to float battleships—even if only as iced tea. Pu'er was another story though. I had heard plenty about its fermented leaves and expected something far more radical.

When I ordered, my server pulled out something she described as a "Pu'er knife" and chipped off some leaves for me from a fist-sized, fragrant, brown block. The first cups were almost clear and had a faint taste of teabag. (Even though there was not one.) As more of these little cups were put in front of me, the liquid in them became darker and the taste more pronounced. It took about fifteen minutes for me to go from novice to tea snob.

By the time the tea I was being served reached the color of dark wood, the flavors started to explode. There was tannin, natural flavors reminiscent of wood and leather, and the distinct cast of fermentation. This was an intense place serving intense stuff. How could you drink alone? How could you down these shot-sized cups of tea without discussing the experience with your fellow club-mates?

The Teaparker was a bastion of seriousness, and conversation was lively and limited to the subject at hand. Any tea reference, no matter

My cup of puer tea, leaves and all, at The Teaparker Teahouse at Penn State University

how obscure, was welcome. How obscure? I mentioned Professor Elemental, the English rapper who sometimes depicts tea drinking in his videos and for the only time in my life, somebody knew who I was talking about.

That little pot of Pu'er was challenging me. What was it all about? How great can tea be? I flipped the menu over and pushed it aside. Instead of the back being blank, there was a premium tea list, a few of which were twenty bucks a pot—a high price for a whole meal at many State College Chinese restaurants.

THE TOMATO FESTIVAL AND FIGHTS IN PITTSTON

LUZERNE COUNTY
35 BROAD ST., PITTSON, PA 18640;
PITTSTONTOMATOFESTIVAL.COM; (570) 655-1424

Pennsylvania does not have the close association with tomato farming that its neighbor New Jersey does. Yet, we grow an awful lot of them, and we surely have a bunch of local dishes that feature them too. For the good people of Pittston, that is enough reason to throw a weekend-long celebration every summer. There is the usual: a parade, a pageant to select the festival queen, and a 5k run. And the less usual: contests for biggest, smallest, ugliest, and most perfect tomatoes. Most unusual of all, there is a huge tomato fight with hundreds of people lobbing rotten, red fruit.

The festival grounds are in downtown Pittston. Walk around and note that the Italian flag is flown proudly here. Restaurants serve the sort of traditional Italian/American food that was popular before average Pennsylvanians started taking vacations in Italy. Shops in the area offer a remarkable variety of imported and artisan ingredients to local customers who obviously know their stuff. It is this very Italian relationship with the tomato that fuels the festival. Tomato as sauce and tomato as metaphor for home cooking as it once was. Not just a vegetable and not just a fruit.

The most unique dish served in Pittston is tripe: strips of poached cow stomach simmered in tomato sauce. Like that Italian flag, tripe here reminds you of local history. Dirt poor and mostly Roman Catholic immigrants came, worked themselves to near death in the mines and factories, and cooked what they could afford in the most delicious way they knew.

Today, the area around Pittston continues to be a magnet for both immigrants and great food and it shows when you see the festival vendors. There is tripe of course, along with pizza, pasta, tacos, burritos, perogies, and all sorts of frozen desserts. An on-site farmers' market specializes in tomatoes and offers lots of other summer produce too; join the locals and stock up.

Then, there is that tomato fight. Held in a large parking lot on Saturday afternoon. Hundreds of people don aprons and goggles and

Real Pittston Tomato Fight action!

then toss case after case of rotten tomatoes at each other while hundreds more watch and cheer them on.

A half-hour before the start, the combatants began to gather in a restaurant parking lot and the sound system began to belt out Lou Monte's "Dominick the Donkey" and Dean Martin's "That's Amore." One teenager told me, "I just got done with the run and I heard there was a fight . . ." There were not just teenagers; parents, fifty-somethings, and even senior citizens were donning goggles and fight tee shirts. Waiting for them were 175 of cases of rotten tomatoes—over five thousand pounds total. All neatly lined up in opposing rows.

Somehow, the crowd divided up into individuals, teams, and even whole families (although small children had to remain on the sidelines). They then picked up handsful of tomatoes, started squeezing them in their fists—the rules required this—and when the horn sounded, they began to throw.

For a few moments, the red stuff was flying everywhere. People were screaming and cheering, and children too small to be in the melee were picking up tomatoes that had landed on the sidelines and hurling them wherever they could. I tried to take pictures, but most of the time, my camera flashed the word "busy" in the viewfinder.

As quickly as it started, it was over and television crews and reporters swarmed into the mob of glop-stained combatants. Many were rolling in the tomato-covered pavement and as I walked around them, their excitement was palpable. It took a few more moments for things to calm down, and then a bulldozer came out, cleaned up the remains, and all that was left was the scent of tomato in the air.

The craziness was contagious. I saw an old friend and announced, "For a few moments there, I truly felt alive!" Later on, I came to my senses and wandered back to the food vendors. A bowl of Pittston-style tripe stew of course, pierogies, and a fruit smoothie were good, but not enough to fill me up. Some local musicians started playing Italian oldies, the judges were getting ready to declare the ugliest tomato, and I was still wondering what else I could eat.

Is this Pennsylvania's best food festival? I think so. It is certainly the most energetic. There is at least a bit of good Italian food here all the time, but it is during the tomato festival that Pittston stops being a quiet, little place wedged between other quiet little places and comes alive, putting its passion for great food—especially great old school, coal country, Italian/American food—on display and crying out until everybody within earshot has had a chance to eat their fill.

VALLEY MILKHOUSE

BERKS COUNTY
92 COVERED BRIDGE RD., OLEY, PA 19547;
VALLEYMILKHOUSE.COM; (610) 816-9813

Everybody remembers that girl back in elementary school, the one who did everything better than anybody else. During my own school days, I did so poorly that I never got to spend much time with the kids who were at that level, but I do remember one thing—their perfect cursive handwriting.

I do not see many examples of that perfect handwriting in my adult life. Most people communicate with me by keyboard. Notes come printed out. Even my wife emails me from her desk, a mere fifteen feet away from mine. But then I saw it at Valley Milkhouse, a cheese maker and farm market in the Oley Valley near Reading. There, on the wall beside the forty-five-gallon steel milk vat, was a to-do list for the day written in the sort of very elegant cursive that only the highest of achievers possess.

I was at Valley Milkhouse for a day-long class. Classes in the art of cheese making seem to come in two different forms. The first one I took (in Lancaster County) included a plastic container of convenience store milk, a bottle of vinegar, and a hot plate, and was conducted at a picnic table. Here at Valley Milkhouse, we began with the calibration of a pH meter and instruction in the handling of live bacterial cultures. There was no middle ground. This was the workshop of an overachiever and I was there as an acolyte.

The day's lesson was in Gouda and we covered the special technique of curd washing that makes it distinctive. There were four of us in the room, three students and Stefanie Angstadt, the owner/cheese maker/instructor. There was no vinegar here! After carefully sanitizing our hands, Stefanie measured out the rennet with a precision I had not seen since I worked in a professional darkroom thirty years before.

There was so much science! Things to measure, things to ask about, things to learn. Fact after fact came at me: what the cows ate, what the rennet was made from, what kept that big steel vat in the middle of the room at the correct temperature. Timing was crucial . . . everything was crucial.

Then Stefanie told us to touch it. She reached down, poked the curd with her fingers and we all did the same. Soon we had our arms in the vat almost elbow deep. And at that moment, we went from pure

The grounds at Valley Milkhouse

science to pure sensuality. The warmth of the curd was an embrace; it was a relationship with food that went far beyond simple cooking. These firmed up bits of dairy protein were loving me back. It was the love of a parent, a child, and a dog too, all in one. People who tell you that you can love food but food cannot love you back have never made cheese this way.

The making of every artisan food has a magic moment that initiates makers into its own private guild. This warm curd was my moment. Soon, those curds were packed into molds and we were sent on our way. A few months on the shelf and they'd lose their sensual magic and become cheese.

Valley Milkhouse is worth a visit for its setting alone. The grounds include an absolutely ancient farmhouse, an actual covered bridge that carries real traffic, and the perfect red painted, wood and stone barn that contains both the milkhouse and the farm shop. Stefanie has the aesthetics right. She makes an elegant product in a beautiful place.

If you are unable to take a cheese class, at least come here for the market. There is cheese, butter, eggs, and maybe local produce or bread in the shop and wandering ducks and dogs to say hello to while you are there. The hardest part is leaving.

WALNUT HILL FARM

MERCER COUNTY
4965 SARANAC DR., SHARPSVILLE, PA 16150;
THEWALNUTHILLFARM.COM; (717) 866-3190

There is a formula for a small, successful, Pennsylvania farm. It is near a big city, or at least a big suburb, and yet it is far enough away to be in a place that appears to be pastoral by comparison. A setting like that will fill the farm store with sophisticated shoppers who will appreciate the hard work that went into producing the very beautiful food that is on display. That works kind of; it works for those farmers lucky enough or rich enough to be near big markets and it leaves the vast majority out in the cold.

Walnut Hill Farm is none of the above. You will find it tucked into the northwest corner of the state and so close to the Ohio line that some of its pastures are on the other side of the border. That makes it a couple of hours drive from Pittsburgh and almost a whole day away from Philadelphia. Yet, from a cow's point of view, its location is perfect. However, if you are heading there from the big city, you are likely facing some time in your car.

Maybe this is not ideal for some of us, but for Michael Kovach, the owner, it is a different story. He sees his farm as being "geographically blessed." When I floundered for a way to describe the area, he suggested "peri-urban." By that he means a mix of old rust belt towns with rural areas in between. It is not suburbia and while the farm itself is countryside, the built-up areas around it are urban, even if they do not have much population anymore.

Despite its rust belt location, Walnut Hill Farm turns out to be idyllic. You will find cattle and sheep grazing on good grass, pigs rooting in the woods, six hundred or so chickens during the summer, and maybe a wayward turkey or two at Thanksgiving. This is a perfect natural environment for meat cultivation and Michael does everything he can to make the most of it. For him, Walnut Hill Farm is his life, his family, and his business all in one.

How does this work? First and foremost, Michael is a cultivator of grass. He provides lush pastures for his livestock. They return the favor in two ways; first, they fertilize the land and encourage plant growth, and second, cattle and sheep eat the grass and those chickens dig for bugs and worms afterward.

Pigs are a bit different. Before they came to live on farms, they were forest dwellers. If they spent their days in pastures alongside the sheep and cattle, you would wind up with some big mud holes and not much grass left for everybody else. In the woods, their digging is moderated by the trees and their diet is supplemented with acorns they forage. It all works out in the end and the result are animals that provide healthy and flavorful meat.

When the farm began, Michael imagined selling whole sides of beef and whole chickens. That may have been a viable business model forty years ago, but not today. Now, people live in much smaller households and simply do not buy that sort of quantity. He even admitted that a whole chicken would be too much for his own three-person family.

With that in mind, they offer properly butchered cuts of the three meats they raise. You can get steaks, chicken legs, or lamb chops if that is your choice. For those of you with the skills and inclination, there are livers, hearts, tongues, and tails. And you can find everything in between too. Do not worry about having to buy too much, packages are about the same size they are at a supermarket. This all means that the farm can stay afloat by selling through their own retail store. In fact, their only marketing is through their social media sites. They are keeping very busy.

Visitors may not come from far away when measured in miles, but many are from another universe psychologically. Children sometimes have trouble telling sheep and pigs apart or express sincere surprise when they learn that fresh eggs are warm when they emerge from the chickens. As Michael told me, "There is nothing more fundamental than food." And it is giving his neighbors and customers a chance to understand it that makes it all worthwhile.

WHOLEY'S MARKET

ALLEGHENY COUNTY
1711 PENN AVE. (STRIP DISTRICT), PITTSBURGH, PA 15222;
WHOLEY.COM; (412) 391-3737

Wholey's Market is an old school, big city market, only bigger. It has an almost block-long red and white striped awning, colorful sidewalk signs advertising what is inside, and employees who really look like they know everything about all those fish you can see as you make your way through the front door.

Start with the crab legs and lobster tails, not by choice, but because you have to walk by them to get to the rest of the store. Most people scoot over to what appears to be the biggest fresh fish counter in Pennsylvania. I saw basa, monkfish, catfish, lake smelts, and at least two dozen other types. This is serious, big-city fish shopping. If you go to a harbor town and try to buy fish off the boats, you would not get this kind of variety.

Monkfish comes from the ocean and the catfish from freshwater farms; almost everything here is sourced from someplace else and somebody has gone to very great lengths to bring them all together here. Even so, many of the experts seemed to be stepping away from the fresh counter and instead looking at the coolers of frozen seafood. There is a bit of wisdom in this, Pittsburgh is far from any ocean. The odds of fish survival are greater this way.

There is a third way to buy fish—live in tanks. Wholey's Market also excels in this area. Farmed catfish and striped bass seem like great choices if you can handle the sight of them being killed and butchered right in front of you.

Walk past the fish section and into the butcher shop. There you will find the selection of a good supermarket meat department along with much larger packages too. I know how easy it is to buy a steak or a pork chop, but the rest is a challenge.

Hidden in the middle of the store and overshadowed by the vast fish and meat displays is a small self-service restaurant. Look carefully before you order—the best is fantastic and the rest should be avoided. Especially stunning was the fried cod. I knew that fried fish was something of an Appalachian specialty but had never seen any that plump and greaseless. The sight of it gave me the courage to

order the most ambitious thing on the menu, a po' boy filled with freshly fried shrimp.

The woman behind the counter described that sandwich with the charm of a professional. She assured me it would have fried shrimp and house-made sauce and would be served on a baguette. When I got it, the shrimp and sauce were sublime and the "baguette" was no more a baguette than it was a killer whale. Instead, it was just a long, soft piece of American bread.

I found the well-hidden dining area and had a perfect moment. No Frenchman would claim responsibility for this bizarre-looking, puffy, and

You can't miss Wholey's Market on the Pittsburgh Strip

chalk-white loaf, but any seafood lover from any country would have downed that impeccable fried shrimp.

Who would think of Pittsburgh as a fish-lovers' town? It makes no sense at all until you visit Wholey's Market. Then, sitting in the dining room with the paper-covered tables, perfect fried seafood in front of you, you understand.

WILDFIRE BREAD

WESTMORELAND COUNTY
3478 ROUTE 711, LIGONIER, PA 15658;
WILDFIREBREAD.COM; (724) 217-2525

If somebody asked you what a person could do with a graduate degree in art, you may say something like, "Teach in a good school" or, "Work in a museum." Nate Johanson had just such a degree and other ideas entirely. His studio projects were huge movable sculptures, and from that he learned how to create big things and transport them. Nate, a passionate sculptor and bread fanatic, saw a handmade, wood-fired oven as a work of art. Using lessons from his school days, he would build one that could be moved from place to place.

With those skills, he created WildFire Bread, a small-town bakery specializing in sourdough loaves. It was his oven on wheels that made it possible. He was able to fabricate and test it at home and then bring it to his shop. When it is time to upgrade the oven, he builds another at home and brings it down after it is tested.

WildFire Bread is in the small town of Ligonier, about fifty miles east of Pittsburgh. It is an upscale sort of place with coffee shops and antique dealers lining a pleasant square. I thought I would find Wild-Fire right downtown and I was wrong. Instead, it was in a small, squat structure about a mile away.

It is a building that looks like it had ice cream somewhere in its history, and it has also been a sandwich shop. However, when it came into Nate's life, it was a wreck. He fixed it all up himself, and without any loans. He jack-hammered and regular hammered too. And then he glazed and painted. Finally, in the end, he brought in his oven-on-wheels, made a porch for it, and opened up his own roadside sour-dough bread shop.

With that, he had become an artist of another sort—a sourdough baker. By definition, sourdough bakers are purists and WildFire Bread is about as pure as they come. They are baked with a house-made sourdough starter and all organic ingredients in that handmade, wood-fired oven.

If you want to be sure of getting his bread, you will have to order in advance and pick up your loaves during the four or so hours a week he's open. Even though there are very few choices, they post a menu on their Facebook page of what is available. You can order one or two—no more—and the week I spoke to Nate, you could choose from Rustic White, Whole Wheat, Caramelized Onion-Poppy, and Double Chocolate Cherry. All sourdough of course.

There are sometimes pretzels—sourdough, wood-fired ones—and that is pretty much what Nate produces. He sells more though; cookies, quiches, soup, and granola—they are made by other local food artisans and while they achieve his level of quality, they may use commercial yeast—so be forewarned.

When the shop opens to the public on Friday afternoons, it is such a popular destination that a farm stand opens in the parking lot. While you are waiting in line for the chance to pick up your order, you can get some seasonal produce and grass-fed beef too.

It all adds up to an artist's life. A hand-crafted space where a man can strive for excellence in one of the most universally consumed foods on the planet. Place an order, come here, and give the bread a try."

Appendix:
Establishments by County

ADAMS COUNTY

Historic Round Barn and Farmers' Market & Oyler's Organic Farms & Market, *Biglerville*
Mister Ed's Elephant Museum & Candy Emporium, *Orrtanna*

ALLEGHENY COUNTY

Beto's Pizza and Restaurant, *Pittsburgh*
Braddock Community Oven, *Pittsburgh*
Enrico Biscotti, *Pittsburgh*
Wholey's Market, *Pittsburgh*

BEAVER COUNTY

Oram's Donut Shop, *Beaver Falls*

BERKS COUNTY

Bowers Chili Pepper Festival, *Bowers*
Daily Loaf Bakery
Deitsch Eck and Restaurant, *Lenhartsville*
Dietrich's Meats & Country Store, *Lenhartsville*
Dove Song Dairy, *Bernville*
Farmhouse Kitchen, The, *West Reading*
Funny Farm Apiary, *Mertztown*
Hay Creek Bread, *Robeson Township*
Longacre's Modern Dairy Bar, *Barto*
Nesting Box Farm Market and Creamery, The, *Kempton*
Rodale Greenhouses at Rodale Institute, The, *Kutztown*
Valley Milkhouse, Cheesemaking Class, *Oley*

BLAIR COUNTY

Clover Creek Cheese Cellar, *Williamsburg*
MarCia's Chocolates, *Altoona*

BUCKS COUNTY

Crossroads Bake Shop, *Doylestown*
Green Zameen Farm, *Perkasie*

CENTRE COUNTY

Penn State Berkey Creamery, *University Park*
State College, Chinatown 2.0, *State College*
Teaparker Tea House, The, *State College*

CHESTER COUNTY

Amazing Acres Goat Dairy
Big Elk Garlic Farm, *Lincoln University*
Bridge Street Chocolates, *Phoenixville*
Himalayan Indian Grocery & Food, *Exton*
Indian Hut, *Exton and Malvern*
Mexican in Kennett Square, *Kennett Square*
Saint Peter's Bakery, *Saint Peter's*

COLUMBIA COUNTY

Rolling Hills Red Deer Farm, *Catawissa*

CRAWFORD COUNTY

Meadville Market House, *Meadville*

CUMBERLAND COUNTY

Eleven Oaks Farms, *Newville*
Josie's German Cafe & Market, *Mechanicsburg*
Talking Breads Bakery, *Mechanicsburg*

DAUPHIN COUNTY

Asia Mall, *Harrisburg*
Broad Street Market, *Harrisburg*
Deep Hollow Forest Farm, *Halifax*
Soul House Cafe, *Harrisburg*

DELAWARE COUNTY

Lancaster County Farmers Market, *Wayne*

FULTON COUNTY

Licking Creek Bend Farm, *Needmore*

GREENE COUNTY

Rising Creek Bakery, *Mount Morris*

HUNTINGDON COUNTY

Standing Stone Coffee, *Huntingdon*

JUNIATA COUNTY

Benner's Butcher Shop, *Thompsontown*
Guante Family Restaurant, *Mifflintown*
Juniata Produce Auction, *Mifflintown*
Ox Dynasty Pennsylvania Hickory Syrup, *Mifflintown*

LACKAWANNA COUNTY

Old Forge: The Pizza Capital of the World, *Old Forge*

LANCASTER COUNTY

Appel Valley Butcher Shop, *Lancaster*
Bird-In-Hand Farm Supply, *Bird-In-Hand*
Central Market, *Lancaster*
Misty Creek Dairy, *Leola*

LEBANON COUNTY

Jigger Shop, The, *Mount Gretna*

LEHIGH COUNTY

Allentown Fairgrounds Market, *Allentown*
Pappy's Orchard and Bakery, *Coopersburg*

LUZERNE COUNTY

Pittston Tomato Festival and Fights, The, *Pittston*

LYCOMING COUNTY

Alabaster Coffee Roaster & Tea Co., *Williamsport*

MERCER COUNTY

Walnut Hill Farm, *Sharpsville*

MIFFLIN COUNTY

Belleville Livestock Auction, The, *Belleville*

MONROE COUNTY

Callie's Candy Kitchen, *Mountainhome*

MONTGOMERY COUNTY

Necessity Farms and Dairy, *Telford*
Sae Han Food Market & To Dam Gol Korean Restaurant, *Blue Bell*

NORTHAMPTON COUNTY

Easton Farmers' Market, *Easton*

NORTHUMBERLAND COUNTY

Masser's Farm Market, *Paxinos*
Sunbury Market House, *Sunbury*

PERRY COUNTY

Red Rabbit Drive In, *Duncannon*

PHILADELPHIA COUNTY

Headhouse Market, *Philadelphia*
John's Roast Pork, *Philadelphia*
La Colombe, *Philadelphia*
Lost Bread Co., *Philadelphia*
Reading Terminal Market, *Philadelphia*
Shane Confectionery, *Philadelphia*

SCHUYLKILL COUNTY

Hometown Farmers Market, *Tamaqua*
Shenandoah Kielbasi, *Shenandoah*

TIOGA COUNTY

Highland Chocolates, *Wellsboro*
Patterson Maple Farms, *Westfield*

UNION COUNTY

Buffalo Valley Produce Auction, *Mifflinburg*

WESTMORELAND COUNTY

Pounds' Turkey Farm, *Leechburg*
WildFire Bread, *Ligonier*

YORK COUNTY

Caputo Brothers Creamery, *Spring Grove*
Haines Shoe House, The, *Hellam*
New Eastern Market, *York*

Index

About the Author

Brian Yarvin has been a commercial photographer for over forty years. Today, his work is represented by Getty Images, StockFood, and Alamy Images. For the past fourteen years, he has been writing as well and is the author of several books. In addition, he has contributed both writing and photography to the *Washington Post, Mothering Magazine,* SeriousEats.com, and *New Jersey Monthly.* He has also taught food photography workshops at the Pennsylvania College of Art and Design in Lancaster.